SQL with PYTHON Version 2.3

For DATA ENGINEERS, DATA ANALYSTS, DATA SCIENTISTS, and who loves Python & SQL

OM PRAKASH SHAKYA
DELHI | INDIA

1

About the Author

Hello Readers, Greetings!

My name is Om Prakash Shakya, working on Software development since year 2010 mostly on Microsoft SQL platform at Data Warehousing/ETL projects using SQL & SSIS as core skills with other tools & languages.

Since 2020, I jumped into the Data Engineering domain and working on PYTHON & SQL mostly with Microsoft Azure as cloud infrastructure.

I am using PYTHON as a core skill now to develop applications and utilities to work with SQL.

My current profile covers the following,

- ✓ IoT data engineering
- ✓ Python code migration to pyspark and vice-versa
- ✓ Data Migration, Processing, Cleansing, Manipulation, Tabularizing
- ✓ Python + SQL, Python + MongoDB
- ✓ Designing & developing tools, utilities, frameworks using Python
- ✓ Research & Development R&D using Python

I have developed a utility package named as 'omshakya', it is available at pypi, you can try it by installing it as,

pip install omshakya

To know more about it visit pypi at https://pypi.org/project/omshakya/
Or the LinkedIn page at "omshakya" a python package

Have experience of data modeling, developing databases, writing complex SQL queries and DDL, DML queries in T-SQL. Collaborating with project owners, stakeholders, SPOCs to discuss the requirements and understand their needs of data to prepare it accordingly.

Rewriting the T-SQL queries to improve the performance, optimizing the packages to reduce the performance hindering tasks/flows, automating the generation of T-SQL scripts for SSIS packages, etc.

Apart from regular activities (above), love to do R&D (Research and development) to solve the problems.
It is the LinkedIn profile link, https://www.linkedin.com/in/om-shakya-49759120

Best of luck,

Thanks to read it.
Om Prakash Shakya

About the book, know the content of the book

This book is about the recipes on PYODBC and SQLAlchemy to work with Microsoft SQL Server databases and its data in table.

Here are various recipes covering almost all the activities that are required by a Data Engineer, Scientist, Analyst or Python Developer.

In future there might be next versions of the book with more advanced topics in easy to use and reference manner as this book has.

Use the content of this book only for reference and modify as per your need.

The book is divided into two sections,

1. PYODBC recipes
2. SQLAlchemy recipies

The topic starts with the heading or title and gives some context about the topic and the lists the complete code block of that topic.

After that there may be one or more approaches or ways that we have implemented in that topic.

Note that there is no guarantee that the Python code or TSQL scripts or any contents are correct and up to date, there might be gaps. The author has executed these codes in their development environment and with specific version of Python, pyodbc, SQLAlchemy, and other related libraries.

It is just the collection of codes/scripts/concepts for easy and personal reference only. Use it as per your knowledge and on your own risk of errors, failures or any other related faults and loss of data is yours; author is not responsible for any kind of harm or loss of data or machine/system failures.

Happy reading!

Disclaimer

Note that there is no guarantee that the Python code or TSQL scripts or any contents are correct and up to date, there might be gaps or mistakes. It is just the collection of scripts/concepts for easy and personal reference only. Use it as per your knowledge and on your own risk of errors, failures or any other related faults and loss of data is yours; **author is not responsible for any kind of harm or loss of data or machine/system failures**.

However, if any of the query is not giving the output or is not working, reader can contact me through contact section at last of the book, author will try to investigate that query as per his availability and reply as soon as possible.

Contents

What is Python?

Python is an interpreted language, it is an object-oriented, high-level programming language.

It provides dynamic semantics, built in high-level data structures, dynamic typing, dynamic binding. It is widely used for Rapid Application Development (RAD), and scripting.

It is simple, easy to learn syntax, it supports modules, packages which helps in program modularity and code re-usability.

Now a days since long time back, python is heavily used in Data Engineering & Data Science field due to very power full packages support and wide & active community all over the world.

For more information read it here at official site of python (what is python?)

What is SQL?

SQL stands for Structured Query Language. It is a standard language for accessing, manipulating, and managing databases specifically RDBMS (relational database management systems).

In this book, we are going to work with Microsoft SQL Server and databases, instead of SQL we will use T-SQL (transact sql) which is specific to Microsoft SQL Server querying.

For more information read it here at the Wikipedia (what is SQL?).

What is VS Code?

VS Code is Visual Studio Code, it is a code editor redefined and optimized for building and debugging modern web and cloud applications.

VS Code is used by Data Engineers also to write applications in Python and other supporting languages.

For more information read it here at official site of VS Code (What is VS Code?).

Install Python

Download the Python with specific version from the official site and install on your machine.

For Windows and macOS, the installers are available, and you must run installer and follow along with steps as per installer.

For Linux/UNIX installation is different so you need to install it accordingly.

Here is the official link to download python (download python).

Install Microsoft SQL Server

To install the Microsoft SQL Server follow the instructions at official site (SQL Server installation guide).

Install VS Code

To install VS Code (Visual Studio Code) follow the instructions at official site (Getting started with Visual Studio Code).

Install required VS Code extensions for Python

To install VS Code extension for Python follow instructions at official site (Quick Start Guide for Python in VS Code).

Create and Setup a Python project

To create and open a Python project follow instructions at official site (Quick Start Guide for Python in VS Code).

What is PYODBC?

A python driver for Sql Server.

pyodbc is a Python open-source module that simplifies access to ODBC databases such as Oracle, MySQL, PostgreSQL, SQL Server, etc.

Use the pyodbc driver to connect to an SQL database from Python code.

PyODBC is community-supported software. Microsoft contributes to the pyODBC open-source community and is an active participant in the repository at https://github.com/mkleehammer/pyodbc/. However, this software doesn't come with Microsoft support.

To know more about pyodbc, read it here (pyodbc).

PYODBC requires ODBC driver to be pre-installed on the machine.

What is ODBC Driver ?

Open Database Connectivity (ODBC) is an open standard Application Programming Interface (API) for accessing a database.

ODBC is a specification for a database API. This API is independent of any one DBMS or operating system; although this manual uses C, the ODBC API is language-independent.

The ODBC API is based on the CLI specifications from Open Group and ISO/IEC. ODBC 3.x fully implements both of these specifications - earlier versions of ODBC were based on preliminary versions of these specifications but did not fully implement them - and adds features commonly needed by developers of screen-based database applications, such as scrollable cursors.

Read more about ODBC Drivers at (What is ODBC?)

How to check whether ODBC is installed or not?

Follow these steps to check whether ODBC driver is installed or not,

1. click on Windows Search textbox or click 'Windows' key
2. Type 'odbc' in search textbox
3. You will see 'ODBC Data sources (32bit/64bit)' under 'Apps', open it
4. Click on 'Drivers' tab and scroll to the bottom, you will see 'ODBC Driver nn for SQL Server'.
5. if not found then it is not installed
6. You can download and install it
7. https://learn.microsoft.com/en-us/sql/connect/odbc/download-odbc-driver-for-sql-server?view=sql-server-ver16

What is SQLALCHEMY?

SQLAlchemy is the Python SQL toolkit and Object Relational Mapper that gives application developers the full power and flexibility of SQL.

Read more about SQLAlchemy here at official site (SQLAlchemy).

Installing PYODBC & SQLALCHEMY

Now install the PYODBC,

If we have created new virtual environment then we can simply install it as,

```
pip install pyodbc
```

If we are using existing venv, then check whether pyodbc is installed or not,

```
pip index versions pyodbc
```

or

```
pip list # pyodbc should be listed if installed
```

Similarly, sqlalchemy can be installed,

```
pip install SQLAlchemy
```

Prepare SQL Database & objects used

To work with this book and code recipes, we must create a database in Microsoft SQL Server either on-premises or in Azure.

Create a database

First, we will create a database named 'db-sql-with-python', to create a database follow the below steps,

1. Open the SSMS (SQL Server Management Studio)
2. Connect to a SQL Server
3. Open a new query window (Click on 'New Query' in SSMS tools or press CTRL+N)
4. Run the following command to create a database

```sql
CREATE DATABASE [db-sql-with-python];
```

5. Choose this new database just created in the list in SSMS toolbar, the available databases or use and run the below command if SQL Server is on local machine,

```sql
USE [db-sql-with-python];
```

6. Comment or delete both the above commands to create database and use database.

Create a table in the database

Continue with above steps till step 6, then run the following SQL script to create a table,
This will create a table with 5 columns mentioned in the CREATE TABLE command.

```sql
CREATE TABLE dbo.customers_tbd(
    ID INT NOT NULL IDENTITY(1,1) PRIMARY KEY,
    customer_name NVARCHAR(50) NOT NULL,
    customer_country NVARCHAR(50) NULL,
    entry_datetime DATETIME NOT NULL DEFAULT GETDATE(),
    is_b2b_customer BIT NOT NULL
)
```

To check whether table created or not, run the below command,

```sql
SELECT *
FROM dbo.customers_tbd
```

Create User Stored Procedures (USPs)

Now, we will create 5 USPs, run the SQL Script of one USP at a time or all at a time,

USP: `dbo.usp_insert_tbd`

This procedure will insert a record into the table.

```sql
CREATE PROCEDURE dbo.usp_insert_tbd(
        @customer_name NVARCHAR(50),
        @customer_country NVARCHAR(50),
        @is_b2b_customer NVARCHAR(50)
)
AS
BEGIN
    SET NOCOUNT ON;
        INSERT INTO dbo.customers_tbd (customer_name, customer_country, is_b2b_customer)
        VALUES (@customer_name, @customer_country, @is_b2b_customer);

        SELECT @@IDENTITY AS 'identity';
END
```

USP: dbo.usp_update_tbd

This USP updates the customer_name for an id.

```sql
CREATE PROCEDURE dbo.usp_update_tbd(
        @id INT,
        @customer_name NVARCHAR(50)
)
AS
BEGIN
        UPDATE dbo.customers_tbd
        SET customer_name = @customer_name
        WHERE ID = @id;
END
```

USP: dbo.usp_getdata_tbd

This USP return multiple result sets.

```sql
CREATE PROCEDURE dbo.usp_getdata_tbd
AS
BEGIN
        SELECT *
        FROM dbo.customers_tbd;

        SELECT COUNT(1) AS total_cutomers, SUM(ID) AS id_sum
        FROM dbo.customers_tbd
```

```
        GROUP BY customer_country;
END
```

USP: dbo.usp_getdata_by_country_tbd

This USP return multiple result sets.

```
CREATE PROCEDURE dbo.usp_getdata_by_country_tbd(
        @country_name NVARCHAR(50)
)
AS
BEGIN
        SELECT *
        FROM dbo.customers_tbd
        WHERE customer_country = @country_name;

        SELECT COUNT(1) AS total_cutomers, SUM(ID) AS id_sum
        FROM dbo.customers_tbd
        GROUP BY customer_country
        HAVING customer_country = @country_name;
END
```

USP: dbo.usp_getcounts_tbd

This USP return a scalar value.

```
CREATE PROCEDURE dbo.usp_getcounts_tbd(
        @counts_output INT OUT
)
AS
BEGIN

        SELECT @counts_output = COUNT(1)
        FROM dbo.customers_tbd;

END
```

These are few of the objects that need to be created in the database that we have created for this learning.

SQL Server Database details required to connect it

To connect a SQL Server from a computer programming language or any scripting language such as Python few of the mandatory information is required to know about that SQL Server and connect it, such as SQL Server name, SQL Server Database name, User ID & password, Driver.

And some other information which will work as a catalyst to work with SQL Server such as encryption, trusting server certificates, connection timeout, and packet size etc.

As we are working here with Microsoft SQL Server & Python and hence, we call the SQL that is Microsoft SQL Server, and the SQL script means Microsoft transact SQL i.e. T-SQL.

All these SQL Server information is used to make a connection string and we will discuss about this in next topic.

Here is the list of all these mandatory and additional information,

Mandatory information:

```
DRIVER = '{ODBC Driver 17 for SQL Server}'
SERVER = 'tcp:sql-some-name.database.windows.net,1493'
DATABASE = 'db-name of database'
USERID = 'user id to login'
PASSWORD = 'password to login'
```

DRIVER is the name of the ODBC driver compatible with your SQL Server version, there are different drivers supporting various SQL Server version.

SERVER is the name of your Microsoft SQL Server, there are different way to provide server details, in above example the name of the SQL Server is 'sql-some-name.database.windows.net' with the 'tcp' port as 1493.

Few more ways to provide SQL Server name are,

```
SERVER = 'localhost\sqlexpress' # for a named instance
SERVER = 'myserver,port' # to specify an alternate port with server name
```

DATABASE is the name of your database in your SQL Server which you are going to connect and access database objects & execute the SQL queries or scripts.

USERID is the user identification to log in into your SQL Server, it is the part of SQL Server login credentials, another part is the password.

PASSWORD is the password to login credentials for the mentioned USERID.

Additional information:

```
ENCRYPT = 'yes'; ### yes or no
TRUSTSERVERCERTIFICATE = 'no' ### yes or no
CONNECTION_TIMEOUT = 1800 ### in seconds
PACKET_SIZE = 4096 ### integer byte size
```

ENCRYPT information is used to specify that the SQL Server connection and communication will be encrypted or not based on your specification i.e. 'yes' or 'no'.

TRUSTSERVERCERTIFICATE specifies whether the server certificate related to security should is trusted or not, mostly it works in case the Microsoft Active Directory integrated security is implemented for the SQL Server access or login. It is set to 'no' when credentials (user id and password) are provided.

CONNECTION_TIMEOUT specifies the time duration in second to timeout in case SQL Server is not responding in that period.

PACKET_SIZE specifies the size of packet to communicate with SQL Server, it is specified in bytes.

Connection string

What is connection string?

The connection string is an expression that contains the parameters required for the applications to connect a database in SQL Server.

Connection string include the server instance, database name, authentication details, and some other settings to communicate with the database server.

Syntax of connection string

The general syntax of connection string is given below,

For mandatory information:

Driver={<driver name>};Server=<server>;Database=<database>;Uid=<username>;Pwd=<password>;
For mandatory information along with additional information:
Driver={<drivername>};Server=<server>;Database=<database>;Uid=<username>;Pwd=<password>;Encrypt=<encrypt>;TrustServerCertificate=<trustservercertificate>;Connection Timeout=<connectiotimeout>;Packet Size=<packetsize>;

From this syntax, it is a combination of key value pairs separated with semi-colon, and hence the keys are:
- Driver
- Server
- Database
- Uid
- Pwd
- Encrypt
- TrustServerCertificate
- Connection Timeout
- Packet Size

The keys are fixed, and values can be parameterized as per different SQL Server information as needed.

Making connection string

There are different ways to make connection string as mentioned below, first we can create python variables with specified values in a python code file as

```python
DRIVER = '{ODBC Driver 17 for SQL Server}'
SERVER = 'tcp:sql-some-name.database.windows.net,1493'
DATABASE = 'db-name of database'
USERID = 'user id to login'
PASSWORD = 'password to login'
### ### additional details
ENCRYPT = 'yes'
TRUSTSERVERCERTIFICATE = 'no'
CONNECTION_TIMEOUT = 1800
PACKET_SIZE = 4096
```

The SQL Server details are highly critical to the business and at most sensitive information and should be handled with highly securable technique, one of the way is keep this information in a special file which is not exposed to the other entity and also make sure that it is not deployed or exposed by your code versioning system such as git and this file should be ignored while working from your local machine.

In a production environment they are handled by senior person and there are various techniques to protect such information for example the environment variables, azure key vault etc.

If we have this information is a special python file which is imported as a module named as 'sqldetails' then we can read it as,

```python
DRIVER = sqldetails.DRIVER
SERVER = sqldetails.SERVER
DATABASE = sqldetails.DATABASE
USERID = sqldetails.USERID
PASSWORD = sqldetails.PASSWORD
### additional details
ENCRYPT = sqldetails.ENCRYPT
TRUSTSERVERCERTIFICATE = sqldetails.TRUSTSERVERCERTIFICATE
CONNECTION_TIMEOUT = sqldetails.CONNECTION_TIMEOUT
PACKET_SIZE = sqldetails.PACKET_SIZE

### different ways to construct connection string

connection_string_1 = f'''DRIVER={DRIVER};
SERVER={SERVER};
DATABASE={DATABASE};
UID={USERID};
```

```python
PWD={PASSWORD}'''

connection_string_2 = f'''Driver={DRIVER};
Server={SERVER};
Database={DATABASE};
Uid={USERID};
Pwd={PASSWORD};
Encrypt=yes;
TrustServerCertificate=no;
Connection Timeout=1800;
Packet Size=4096;'''

connection_string_3 = f'''DRIVER={{ODBC Driver 17 for SQL Server}};
SERVER={SERVER};
DATABASE={DATABASE};
UID={USERID};
PWD={PASSWORD}'''

connection_string_4 = 'DRIVER={SQL Server};SERVER=' + SERVER + ';DATABASE=' +
DATABASE + ';UID=' + USERID + ';PWD='+ PASSWORD

connection_string_5 = "Driver={ODBC Driver 17 for SQL
Server};Server=tcp:#SERVER#.database.windows.net,1433;Database=#DB#;Uid=#USERID#;Pwd=
#PWD#;Encrypt=yes;TrustServerCertificate=no;Connection Timeout=1800;Packet
Size=4096;"

connection_string_6 = (connection_string_5.replace('#SERVER#', SERVER)
    .replace('#DB#', DATABASE)
    .replace('#USERID#', USERID)
    .replace('#PWD#', PASSWORD))
```

Above are the six different ways to construct a connection string, few of them may have slight differences if you noticed it. This is up to you how you create a connection string with required SQL Server details.

How to avoid creating connection string every time?

How to avoid creating connection string every time in different modules or code files or places whenever we intend to perform SQL activities?

The best way to implement this is that we should follow the Object-Oriented Programming (OOPs) and apply OOPs concepts.

Another way is we can create the Python modules. Here is the example using modules.
Let say we have stored the connection string related information in a file:

```python
### mandatory details
DRIVER = '{ODBC Driver 17 for SQL Server}'
SERVER = 'tcp: sql-some-name.database.windows.net,1433'
DATABASE = 'db-name'
USERID = 'userid'
PASSWORD = 'strong password'
### additional details
ENCRYPT = 'yes';
TRUSTSERVERCERTIFICATE = 'no'
CONNECTION_TIMEOUT = 1800
PACKET_SIZE = 4096
```

Then we create a module file with a function/method get_odbc_connection_string() as,

```python
import __connection_details_sqlserver as __sqldetails

def get_odbc_connection_string():

    ### ### read details
    ### at least the following details
    DRIVER = __sqldetails.DRIVER
    SERVER = __sqldetails.SERVER
    DATABASE = __sqldetails.DATABASE
    USERID = __sqldetails.USERID
    PASSWORD = __sqldetails.PASSWORD
    ### additional details
    ENCRYPT = __sqldetails.ENCRYPT
    TRUSTSERVERCERTIFICATE = __sqldetails.TRUSTSERVERCERTIFICATE
    CONNECTION_TIMEOUT = __sqldetails.CONNECTION_TIMEOUT
    PACKET_SIZE = __sqldetails.PACKET_SIZE

    ### prepare connection string here
    connection_string = f'''Driver={DRIVER};
        Server={SERVER};
        Database={DATABASE};
        Uid={USERID};
        Pwd={PASSWORD};
        Encrypt=yes;
        TrustServerCertificate=no;
```

```
        Connection Timeout=1800;
        Packet Size=4096;'''

    return connection_string
```

I hope the above module and its function is super easy and it can be extended to handle as per your requirements. The function can be parameterized for a different database or even different SQL Server and other objects.

Kindly remember these modules, we will be using them frequently in next topics and overall subsequent code recipes.

PYODBC Code recipes

1. Preparing connection string and making connection

1.1.   preparing SQL server connection string

To prepare the SQL server connection string read the following topics above.

- Making connection string
- How to avoid creating connection string every time?

1.2.   making connection to SQL Server

Using PYODBC library we can create the connection to the SQL Server. There are the following 2 approaches or ways to create the connection.

- ✓ approach: 1 - explicit calls
- ✓ approach: 2 - using 'with' statement

pyodbc_01_02_making_connection.py

```python
import pyodbc
import __connection_string_utils as csutils


connection_string = csutils.get_odbc_connection_string()


print('connecting to sql ...\n')
##################################################################
##### approach: 1 - explicit calls
##################################################################
try:
    _connection = pyodbc.connect(connection_string)
    print('connection successful,')
    print(_connection)

    ### create cursor to execute commands
    _cursor = _connection.cursor()

    ### execute the sql commands here
    ### commit the command if required

    ### then close the cursor and connection
    _cursor.close()
    _connection.close()
```

```python
except Exception as ex:
    print(f'ERROR: {ex}')


################################################################
##### approach: 2 - using 'with' statement
################################################################
# using ''with' the connection is automatically closed when leaving the 'with' block
with pyodbc.connect(connection_string) as _connection:
    print('connection successful,')
    print(_connection)

    ### create cursor to execute commands
    _cursor = _connection.cursor()

    ### execute the sql commands here
    ### commit the command if required

    ### then close the cursor and connection
    ### connection is automatically closed
print("now it is out of 'with' block")
```

In this code recipes, notice the line,

```python
import __connection_string_utils as csutils
```

It is importing a module which we have created above to get the SQL Server connection string.

And in import pyodbc, pyodbc is the standard module which we installed a library called pyodbc. `pyodbc.connect(connection_string)` returns a connection object if SQL Server is connected successfully using the connection string passed to connect() method, otherwise it will raise an exception in case any error is occurred.

Then we can create a 'cursor' object which is used to perform various SQL activities.
```python
_cursor = _connection.cursor()
```

Cursor is the database cursor; it has the capabilities to perform SQL operations and provides the context of the operation being executed.

After performing the SQL operation there is possibility to commit the transactions carried out by SQL operation such as update, delete or any DDL commands broadly is database state is changing by your operation. The Select command means reading data does not change the state of database and in this case, there is no need to commit the transaction.

To commit the transaction a commit() of connection is called; we will see and discuss in next possible topic.

At last, the cursor needs to be closed the connection as well should also be closed.

```
_cursor.close()
_connection.close()
```

While using the 'with' statement the closing of connection is taken care automatically and the corresponding cursor is also closed during this automation capability of 'with' statement.

2.0. inserting data into SQL Database table

In this recipe, we will discuss about inserting data into SQL Database table. As we know from SQL that data can be inserted into a table by a SQL insert statement.

This insert statement could be a plain SQL query/command or it can be wrapped into a SQL stored procedure also known as user stored procedures (USP).

The insert statement contains the name of the table, the columns, and the values to be inserted. We can insert a single record or multiple records. The multiple records can be represented by a list or list or tuple in python.

The values to be inserted into row column are passed as parameters. There are different ways or approaches to pass the parameters.

Here we will discuss the following approaches,

- ✓ approach: 1 - with named parameters
- ✓ approach: 2 - with parameters as list
- ✓ approach: 3 - with parameters as tuple
- ✓ approach: 4 - with parameters as list of tuples (multiple rows)
- ✓ approach: 5 - with loop on dataframe and named parameters (multiple rows)
- ✓ approach: 6 - with dataframe rows as list of tuple (multiple rows)

pyodbc_02_insert.py

```python
import pyodbc
from random import randrange
import pandas as pd
import __connection_string_utils as csutils


# ### prepare/get the connection string
connection_string = csutils.get_odbc_connection_string()
```

```python
print('connect to sql and insert data ...\n')
_connection = None
_cursor = None
try:
    ### create connection and cursor, and set autocommit to False
    _connection = pyodbc.connect(connection_string)
    _connection.autocommit = False
    _cursor = _connection.cursor()

    ### execute the sql commands here

    sql = """INSERT INTO dbo.customers_tbd (customer_name, customer_country, is_b2b_customer)
        VALUES (?, ?, ?);"""


    ############################################################
    ##### approach: 1 - with named parameters
    ############################################################


    customername = 'B'
    customercountry = 'Argentina'
    is_b2b_customer = False

    _cursor.execute(sql, customername, customercountry, is_b2b_customer)
    print(f'approach 1 executed.')


    ############################################################
    ##### approach: 2 - with parameters as list
    ############################################################


    num = randrange(9)
    customername1 = customername + str(num)

    num = randrange(9)
    customername2 = customername + str(num)

    num = randrange(9)
    customername3 = customername + str(num)

    ### parameters as list
    params_as_list = [customername1, customercountry, is_b2b_customer]

    _cursor.execute(sql, params_as_list)
    print(f'approach 2 executed.')
```

```python
###############################################################
##### approach: 3 - with parameters as tuple
###############################################################

params_as_tuple = (customername2, customercountry, is_b2b_customer)

_cursor.execute(sql, params_as_tuple)
print(f'approach 3 executed.')


###############################################################
##### approach: 4 - with parameters as list of tuples (multiple rows)
###############################################################

params_as_list_of_tuple = [(customername2, customercountry, is_b2b_customer)
                          ,(customername3, customercountry, is_b2b_customer)]

_cursor.executemany(sql, params_as_list_of_tuple)
print(f'approach 4 executed.')


###############################################################
##### approach: 5 - with loop on dataframe and named parameters (multiple rows)
###############################################################

data = {'custname': ['mukesh', 'alex', 'robin'],
        'country': ['India', 'Russia', 'China'],
        'isb2b':[True, False, True],
        'currency':['indian rupee', 'Russian Ruble', 'Chinese Yuan']}

df = pd.DataFrame(data)
print(df)

print('\niterating df rows ...')
for index, row in df.iterrows():
    _cursor.execute(sql, row.custname, row.country,row.isb2b)

print(f'approach 5 executed.')


###############################################################
##### approach: 6 - with dataframe rows as list of tuple (multiple rows)
###############################################################

df_only_needed = df[['custname', 'country', 'isb2b']]

row_as_list_of_tuple = [tuple(row) for idx, row in df_only_needed.iterrows()]
```

```python
    _cursor.executemany(sql, row_as_list_of_tuple)
    print(f'approach 6 executed.')

    ### commit the command if required
    _connection.commit()

    ### then close the cursor and connection
    _cursor.close()
    _connection.close()

except Exception as ex:
    print(f'ERROR: {ex}')
```

In the above recipe to insert the data into database table, we have created a connection and cursor and then we have declared a SQL statement to insert the data into database table as

```python
sql = """INSERT INTO dbo.customers_tbd (customer_name, customer_country, is_b2b_customer)
        VALUES (?, ?, ?);"""
```

In this statement 'dbo.customers_tbd' is the table name, and customer_name, customer_country, is_b2b_customer are the column names. Then VALUES (?, ?, ?).

Here the question marks are the place holders to put the values by parameters. There are 3 columns mentioned and so are 3 place holders. This insert statement is the valid SQL insert query.

Cursor has a method named execute() which is used to execute a SQL statement and this statement can be any valid SQL query for the SQL server and database.

The syntax of the execute() method is

cursor.execute(sql, * params)

The first argument of execute() is sql and another argument could be zero or more parameters as required and hence if the SQL statement does not have any placeholder then there is no need to pass the parameters and we can simply call it like cursor.execute(sql).

Now we will discuss each approach separately,

approach: 1 - with named parameters

The name parameters are not any standardized terminology but only the python variable declaration and passing them in the correct order. We can pass the plain values explicitly also.

Here in this approach we have declared the required parameters and passing them in execute() method as

```
customername = 'B'
customercountry = 'Argentina'
is_b2b_customer = False

_cursor.execute(sql, customername, customercountry, is_b2b_customer)
```

Notice variables passed after sql.

approach: 2 - with parameters as list

In this approach we are creating a python list and passing it as a param along with sql in execute() method as

```
params_as_list = [customername1, customercountry, is_b2b_customer]

_cursor.execute(sql, params_as_list)
```

The variable params_as_list is a list of 3 other variables.

approach: 3 - with parameters as tuple

In this approach we are creating a python tuple and passing it as a param along with sql in execute() method as

```
params_as_tuple = (customername2, customercountry, is_b2b_customer)

_cursor.execute(sql, params_as_tuple)
```

The variable params_as_tuple is a tuple with 3 elements.

approach: 4 - with parameters as list of tuples (multiple rows)

In this approach we are inserting multiple records. To insert multiple records the same SQL insert statement is used and we have to pass the column values for multiple records.

Here we are creating a list of tuples. One tuple represents a single record and so list of tuples will form multiple records and this list of tuples will be passed along with sql into executemany() method as

```
params_as_list_of_tuple = [(customername2, customercountry, is_b2b_customer)
                          ,(customername3, customercountry, is_b2b_customer)]


_cursor.executemany(sql, params_as_list_of_tuple)
```

The variable params_as_list_of_tuple is a list of tuples and contains 2 tuples that is 2 records to be inserted into database table.
Notice that we have used the executemany() method of cursor instead of execute() method.

approach: 5 - with loop on dataframe and named parameters (multiple rows)

In this approach we are inserting multiple records and it shows different way to achieve this. The interesting part is that we have pandas dataframe with multiple records.

```
data = {'custname': ['mukesh', 'alex', 'robin'],
        'country': ['India', 'Russia', 'China'],
        'isb2b':[True, False, True],
        'currency':['indian rupee', 'Russian Ruble', 'Chinese Yuan']}

df = pd.DataFrame(data)
print(df)
```

To insert multiple records, we will iterate over the dataframe and will insert a record at a time. In a loop we are accessing row and its required column and passing them along with sql into execute() method as

```
for index, row in df.iterrows():
    _cursor.execute(sql, row.custname, row.country,row.isb2b)
```

approach: 6 - with dataframe rows as list of tuple (multiple rows)

In this approach we are inserting multiple records and it shows different way to achieve this. The interesting part is that we have pandas dataframe with multiple records and we will call executemany() method of cursor.

```python
df_only_needed = df[['custname', 'country', 'isb2b']]


row_as_list_of_tuple = [tuple(row) for idx, row in df_only_needed.iterrows()]


_cursor.executemany(sql, row_as_list_of_tuple)
```

In the following line, we have used python comprehension to create list of tuples and passing it as parameter along with sql in executemany() method of the cursor.

These were 6 different approaches to insert records into database table using execute() and executemany() methods of cursor and we can insert either single or multiple records.

After calling execute() or executemany() method the task of data insertion is done but we have changed the state of database table and database so we have to commit our transaction performed through cursor. We can achieve this by calling commit() method of connection as

```python
_connection.commit()
```

And then we should close the cursor and connection as

```python
_cursor.close()
_connection.close()
```

3.0. Updating data in SQL Database table

In this recipe, we will discuss about updating the existing data in SQL Database table. As we know from SQL that data can be updated in a table by a SQL update statement.

This update statement could be a plain SQL query/command or it can be wrapped into a SQL stored procedure also known as user stored procedures (USP).

The update statement contains the name of the table, the column, and the value to be updated. We can update a single record or multiple records.

The new values to update the existing column values are passed as parameters. There are different ways or approaches to pass the parameters.

Here we will discuss the following approaches,

- ✓ approach: 1 - with hard coded update
- ✓ approach: 2 - with named or explicit parameters
- ✓ approach: 3 - with parameters as list
- ✓ approach: 4 - with parameters as tuple
- ✓ approach: 5 - with parameters as list of tuples (update multiple rows)
- ✓ approach: 6 - with loop on dataframe and named parameters (update multiple rows)
- ✓ approach: 7 - with dataframe rows as list of tuple (update multiple rows)

pyodbc_03_update.py

```python
import pyodbc
import pandas as pd
import __connection_string_utils as csutils


# ### prepare/get the connection string
connection_string = csutils.get_odbc_connection_string()


print('connect to sql and update data ...\n')
_connection = None
_cursor = None
try:
    ### create connection and cursor, and set autocommit to False
    _connection = pyodbc.connect(connection_string)
    _connection.autocommit = False
    _cursor = _connection.cursor()


    ### execute the sql commands here


    ############################################################
    ##### approach: 1 - with hard coded update
    ############################################################

    sql = """UPDATE dbo.customers_tbd
    SET customer_country = 'Mexico'
    WHERE customer_name = 'alex';"""


    row_count = _cursor.execute(sql).rowcount
    print(f'approach 1 executed. rows affected: {row_count}')


    ############################################################
```

```python
##### approach: 2 - with named or explicit parameters
################################################################

sql = """UPDATE dbo.customers_tbd
SET is_b2b_customer = ?,
    customer_country = ?
WHERE ID = ?;"""

is_b2b_customer = True
customercountry = 'China'
id = 3

row_count = _cursor.execute(sql, is_b2b_customer, customercountry, id).rowcount
print(f'approach 2 executed. rows affected: {row_count}')


################################################################
##### approach: 3 - with parameters as list
##### approach: 4 - with parameters as tuple
################################################################

# we can execute update statement similar to insert
# both the approaches 3 & 4 to pass params will work

# parameters as list
params_as_list = [is_b2b_customer, customercountry, id]

# parameters as tuple
params_as_tuple = (is_b2b_customer, customercountry, id)

print(f'approach 3 bypassed')
print(f'approach 4 bypassed')


################################################################
##### approach: 5 - with parameters as list of tuples (update multiple rows)
################################################################

sql = """UPDATE dbo.customers_tbd
    SET is_b2b_customer = ?,
        customer_country = ?
    WHERE ID = ?;"""

params_as_list_of_tuple = [(False, 'Singapore', 9),
                           (False, 'Singapore', 10)]

_cursor.executemany(sql, params_as_list_of_tuple)
```

```python
print(f'approach 5 executed.')

###############################################################
##### approach: 6 - with loop on dataframe and named parameters (update multiple rows)
###############################################################

data = {'id': [6, 8],
        'custname': ['mukesh', 'robin'],
        'custname_new': ['mukesh kumar', 'robin singh'],
        'country': ['indonesia', 'indonesia'],
        'currency':['Indonesian Rupiah', 'Indonesian Rupiah']}

df = pd.DataFrame(data)
print(df)

sql = """UPDATE dbo.customers_tbd
    SET customer_name = ?
    WHERE customer_name = ?
    AND ID = ?;"""

print('\niterating df rows ...')
for index, row in df.iterrows():
    _cursor.execute(sql, row.custname_new, row.custname, row.id)

print(f'approach 6 executed.')

###############################################################
##### approach: 7 - with dataframe rows as list of tuple (update multiple rows)
###############################################################

data = {'id': [6, 8],
        'custname': ['mukesh', 'robin'],
        'custname_new': ['mukesh kumar updated', 'robin singh updated'],
        'country': ['singapore', 'singapore'],
        'currency':['sgd', 'sgd']}

df = pd.DataFrame(data)
print(df)

sql = """UPDATE dbo.customers_tbd
SET customer_name = ? ,
    customer_country = ?
WHERE ID = ?;"""

df_only_needed = df[['custname_new', 'country', 'id']]
```

33

```python
row_as_list_of_tuple = [tuple(row) for idx, row in df_only_needed.iterrows()]

_cursor.executemany(sql, row_as_list_of_tuple)
print(f'approach 7 executed.')

### commit the command if required
_connection.commit()

### then close the cursor and connection
_cursor.close()
_connection.close()

except Exception as ex:
    print(f'ERROR:\n{ex}')
```

approach: 1 - with hard coded update

In this approach we will see an update statement in SQL in which the values to be updated are hard coded and so the SQL statement does not need any parameters. We can execute this statement using execute() method of cursor.

We will also see that how we can check that how many records were updated or modified by the SQL statement using rowcount property of the cursor.

The update SQL statement and the execution call is shown below,

```python
sql = """UPDATE dbo.customers_tbd
SET customer_country = 'Mexico'
WHERE customer_name = 'alex';"""

row_count = _cursor.execute(sql).rowcount
print(f'approach 1 executed. rows affected: {row_count}')
```

In this SQL update statement, we are updated customer_country value by 'Mexico' for the record where the customer_name is 'alex' in the dbo.customers_tbd table.

If there is no record with 'alex' in customer_name then no records will be updated, if there is only one record then that record will be updated and if there are multiple records then those records will be updated.

The 'rowcount' property of the cursor returns the number of rows or records updated or affected or modified which ever terminology you understand.

approach: 2 - with named or explicit parameters

In this approach we will have a SQL update statement with the place holders marked by question mark (?) so we must pass that number of parameters in the same order (top to bottom, left to right in SQL query) explicitly.

Let say we have the following SQL update query/statement in which we want to update 2 columns (is_b2b_customer, customer_country) for a particular value of ID column.

```
sql = """UPDATE dbo.customers_tbd
SET is_b2b_customer = ?,
    customer_country = ?
WHERE ID = ?;"""
```

So, there are 3 place holders and hence 3 parameters are required to execute this statement. This can be achieved as

```
is_b2b_customer = True
customercountry = 'China'
id = 3

row_count = _cursor.execute(sql, is_b2b_customer, customercountry, id).rowcount
print(f'approach 2 executed. rows affected: {row_count}')
```

Notice the column data type of 'is_b2b_customer' is bit or Boolean in SQL and in python it is mapped to bool.
Also, we are getting rows affected using 'rowcount'. As ID is the identity column so there may be maximum 1 record in the table if that is available, in case ID value does not match or exists in table then there will be no record to update.

approach: 3 - with parameters as list
approach: 4 - with parameters as tuple

The approaches 3 and 4 are like the approaches in 'inserting data into SQL Database table' and they will work fine if you refer those.

We can easily create the list of parameters and tuple of parameters as

```
# parameters as list
params_as_list = [is_b2b_customer, customercountry, id]


# parameters as tuple
```

```
params_as_tuple = (is_b2b_customer, customercountry, id)
```

and these can be passed into execute() method.
Kindly refer the said topic.

approach: 5 - with parameters as list of tuples (update multiple rows)

In this approach we try to update multiple records in the table, so we need to pass the collection of required parameters as a list of tuples. One tuple will represent a combination of individual values for a single record and hence list of tuples will represent multiple records or collection.

We have the following SQL update statement, and it needs 3 values for a single record.

```
sql = """UPDATE dbo.customers_tbd
    SET is_b2b_customer = ?,
        customer_country = ?
    WHERE ID = ?;"""
```

For multiple records we can prepare list of tuples and pass it to exeutemany() method of cursor as

```
params_as_list_of_tuple = [(False, 'Singapore', 9),
                           (False, 'Singapore', 10)]

_cursor.executemany(sql, params_as_list_of_tuple)
print(f'approach 5 executed.')
```

Notice we have used executemany() method to update multiple records by the SQL update statement.

approach: 6 - with loop on dataframe and named parameters (update multiple rows)

Let say we have a pandas dataframe with multiple rows and we want to update the new values of few columns based on some conditions. We can update it.

We have a pandas dataframe like this,

```
data = {'id': [6, 8],
        'custname': ['mukesh', 'robin'],
        'custname_new': ['mukesh kumar', 'robin singh'],
        'country': ['indonesia', 'indonesia'],
        'currency':['Indonesian Rupiah', 'Indonesian Rupiah']}
```

```
df = pd.DataFrame(data)
print(df)
```

Notice, the above dataframe has 'custname' column and 'custname_new' column, some how based on business logic or via some reference we have corrected the values for 'customer_name' column in dbo.customers_tbd table.

And we want to replace the existing values by the values in 'custname_new' in dataframe for corresponding ID.

So, we have prepared this SQL update statement where the customer_name values will be updated by new values in 'custname_new' in dataframe as

```
sql = """UPDATE dbo.customers_tbd
    SET customer_name = ?
    WHERE customer_name = ?
    AND ID = ?;"""
```

To achieve this, we must iterate over the dataframe and access the row and required column and pass the parameters as expected.

NOTE: The first parameter in SQL query needs the value from 'custname_new' from dataframe and second parameter need the existing value of customer_name which is 'custname' in dataframe and the third parameter is 'id' of dataframe.

```
print('\niterating df rows ...')
for index, row in df.iterrows():
    _cursor.execute(sql, row.custname_new, row.custname, row.id)


print('approach 6 executed.')
```

approach: 7 - with dataframe rows as list of tuple (update multiple rows)

In this approach we are trying to update multiple records in SQL database table, and we have a dataframe prepared with all the required values to be passed as parameters.

As we have seen in above section 'inserting data into sql database table', multiple records can be updated also.

Let's look at the dataframe,

```python
data = {'id': [6, 8],
        'custname': ['mukesh', 'robin'],
        'custname_new': ['mukesh kumar updated', 'robin singh updated'],
        'country': ['singapore', 'singapore'],
        'currency':['sgd', 'sgd']}

df = pd.DataFrame(data)
print(df)
```

Notice that the dataframe has multiple rows and multiple columns, and we want to update the customer_name and customer_country for the particular ID.

The required SQL update statement is given below, and it has 3 place holders marked so needs 3 parameters.

```python
sql = """UPDATE dbo.customers_tbd
SET customer_name = ? ,
    customer_country = ?
WHERE ID = ?;"""
```

As in dataframe above, there are multiple columns, and we must access only the required columns in the same order and iterate over the rows to create the list of tuples.

```python
df_only_needed = df[['custname_new', 'country', 'id']]
row_as_list_of_tuple = [tuple(row) for idx, row in df_only_needed.iterrows()]

_cursor.executemany(sql, row_as_list_of_tuple)
print(f'approach 7 executed.')
```

Notice, we have again called the executemany() as we are passing multiple parameters to update multiple records.

These were 7 different approaches to update records in database table using execute() and executemany() methods of cursor and we can update either single or multiple records.

After calling execute() or executemany() method the task of data updation is done but we have changed the state of database table and database so we have to commit our transaction performed through cursor. We can achieve this by calling commit() method of connection as

```
    _connection.commit()
```

And then we should close the cursor and connection as

```
    _cursor.close()
    _connection.close()
```

4.0. Deleting data in SQL Database table

In this recipe, we will discuss about deleting the records from SQL Database table. As we know from SQL that data can be deleted in a table by a SQL delete statement.

This delete statement could be a plain SQL query/command or it can be wrapped into a SQL stored procedure also known as user stored procedures (USP).

The delete statement contains the name of the table, and the condition to specify which records must be deleted.
We can delete a single record or multiple records or all the records. To delete all the records the condition must be omitted from the delete statement.

The condition is built upon the columns of the table and in SQL delete statement, the value of the columns can be parameterized. There are different ways or approaches to pass the parameters.

Here we will discuss the following approaches,

- ✓ approach: 1 - with hard coded delete
- ✓ approach: 2 - with named or explicit parameters
- ✓ approach: 3 - with parameters as list of tuples (delete multiple rows)
- ✓ approach: 4,5,6,7 take reference from 3.0 update

pyodbc_04_delete.py

```python
import pyodbc
import __connection_string_utils as csutils


# ### prepare/get the connection string
connection_string = csutils.get_odbc_connection_string()


print('connect to sql and delete data ...\n')
_connection = None
```

```python
_cursor = None
try:
    ### create connection and cursor, and set autocommit to False
    _connection = pyodbc.connect(connection_string)
    _connection.autocommit = False
    _cursor = _connection.cursor()

    ### execute the sql commands here

    ###############################################################
    ##### approach: 1 - with hard coded delete
    ###############################################################

    sql = """DELETE FROM dbo.customers_tbd
    WHERE customer_name LIKE 'B%';"""

    row_count = _cursor.execute(sql).rowcount
    print(f'approach 1 executed. rows affected: {row_count}')


    ###############################################################
    ##### approach: 2 - with named or explicit parameters
    ###############################################################

    sql = """DELETE FROM dbo.customers_tbd
    WHERE customer_country = ?
    AND customer_name = ?
    AND ID = ?;"""

    customercountry = 'Mexico'
    custname = 'alex'
    id = 7

    row_count = _cursor.execute(sql, customercountry, custname, id).rowcount
    print(f'approach 2 executed. rows affected: {row_count}')


    ###############################################################
    ##### approach: 3 - with parameters as list of tuples (delete multiple rows)
    ###############################################################

    sql = """DELETE FROM dbo.customers_tbd
    WHERE is_b2b_customer = ?
    AND ID = ?;"""

    params_as_list_of_tuple = [(False, 8), (True, 6)]
```

```
    _cursor.executemany(sql, params_as_list_of_tuple)
    print(f'approach 3 executed.')



    ################################################################
    ##### NOTES
    # we have covered the following 3 approaches
    ##### approach: 1 - with hard coded update
    ##### approach: 2 - with named or explicit parameters
    ##### approach: 3 - with parameters as list of tuples (update multiple rows)

    # the rest approaches can followed along with as in 'insert' or 'update'
    ##### approach: 4 - with parameters as list
    ##### approach: 5 - with parameters as tuple
    ##### approach: 6 - with loop on dataframe and named parameters (update multiple rows)
    ##### approach: 7 - with dataframe rows as list of tuple (update multiple rows)
    ################################################################

    ### commit the command if required
    _connection.commit()

    ### then close the cursor and connection
    _cursor.close()
    _connection.close()

except Exception as ex:
    print(f'could not connect\n{ex}')
```

approach: 1 - with hard coded delete

In this approach we will see a delete statement in SQL, which is used to delete all the records where the customer_name starts with the letter 'B'.

```
sql = """DELETE FROM dbo.customers_tbd
WHERE customer_name LIKE 'B%';"""
```

In the condition this is hard coded and so this does not need any parameters. We can execute this statement using execute() method of cursor.

We will also see that how we can check that how many records were delete or affected by the SQL statement using rowcount property of the cursor.

```
row_count = _cursor.execute(sql).rowcount
print(f'approach 1 executed. rows affected: {row_count}')
```

approach: 2 - with named or explicit parameters

In this approach the following delete SQL statement is used,

```
sql = """DELETE FROM dbo.customers_tbd
WHERE customer_country = ?
AND customer_name = ?
AND ID = ?;"""
```

As we can see that, we want to delete the records that matches the 3 conditions with AND Boolean operator and so there are 3 parameters required. It is a case of multiple parameters and there are 3 placeholders to accept their values.

We are declaring the 3 variables that will be passed along with delete SQL statement into execute() method,

```
customercountry = 'Mexico'
custname = 'alex'
id = 7

row_count = _cursor.execute(sql, customercountry, custname, id).rowcount
print(f'approach 2 executed. rows affected: {row_count}')
```

Notice, we have used the rowcount property to get the number of rows that were deleted.

approach: 3 - with parameters as list of tuples (delete multiple rows)

In this approach we want to delete the multiple records with different set of conditions so multiple values of the parameters are used.
First investigate the delete statement,

```
sql = """DELETE FROM dbo.customers_tbd
WHERE is_b2b_customer = ?
AND ID = ?;"""
```

As per delete SQL statement the condition is that if the is_b2b_customer & ID matches the parameter values than delete it, and we will try to pass different set of parameter values.

This is passed as list of tuples,

```python
params_as_list_of_tuple = [(False, 8), (True, 6)]

_cursor.executemany(sql, params_as_list_of_tuple)
print(f'approach 3 executed.')
```

Notice, we have called the executemany() as we are passing multiple parameters to update multiple records.

approach: 4,5,6,7 take reference from 3.0 update section

we have covered the following 3 approaches to delete the records from the SQL database table.

- approach: 1 - with hard coded update
- approach: 2 - with named or explicit parameters
- approach: 3 - with parameters as list of tuples (update multiple rows)

The rest approaches can follow along with as in 'insert' or 'update' sections.

- approach: 4 - with parameters as list
- approach: 5 - with parameters as tuple
- approach: 6 - with loop on dataframe and named parameters (update multiple rows)
- approach: 7 - with dataframe rows as list of tuple (update multiple rows)

After calling execute() or executemany() method the task of data deletion is done but we have changed the state of database table and database so we have to commit our transaction performed through cursor. We can achieve this by calling commit() method of connection as

```python
_connection.commit()
```

And then we should close the cursor and connection as

```python
_cursor.close()
_connection.close()
```

5.1. Reading/Selecting data from SQL Database table and exploring fetchall() function

In this recipe, we will discuss about reading the records from SQL Database table. As we know from SQL that data can be read from a table by a SQL select statement.

This select statement could be a plain SQL query/command or it can be wrapped into a SQL stored procedure also known as user stored procedures (USP).

The statement could be to read all the records or read the records that matches some condition which is also known as filtering the records and it is specified using where clause in SQL.

If a select statement has some condition, then it may or may not require the parameters whichever is possible.

There are different ways or approaches to read or select the data and we will discuss few of them here.

Specifically we will explore the fetchall() method of the cursor to get the results of a SQL Query. The fetchall() method should be used while reading or selecting data from SQL database table using a plain SQL or a user defined stored procedure (USP).

Here we will discuss the following topics,

- ✓ explore fetchall() results: 1- type of result and print result
- ✓ explore fetchall() results: 2- loop through result and accessing columns by index
- ✓ explore fetchall() results: 3- loop through result and accessing columns by name
- ✓ explore cursor description: 4- type of description, see it and get column names
- ✓ explore fetchall() results: 5- convert to pandas dataframe

pyodbc_05_01_select_fetchall.py

```python
import pyodbc
import pandas as pd
import __connection_string_utils as csutils


# ### prepare/get the connection string
connection_string = csutils.get_odbc_connection_string()

print('connect to sql and select/read data ...\n')
_connection = None
_cursor = None


try:
    ### create connection and cursor, and set autocommit to False
    _connection = pyodbc.connect(connection_string)
```

```python
    _connection.autocommit = False
    _cursor = _connection.cursor()


    ### execute the sql commands here

    sql = "SELECT name, name AS aliased_name, name AS [spaced name] FROM sys.databases;"
    _cursor.execute(sql)


    rows = _cursor.fetchall()


    #############################################################
    ##### explore fetchall() results: 1- type of result and print result
    #############################################################
    print('\n1- type of result and print rows...')
    print(f'type of result: {type(rows)}')
    print(rows)


    #############################################################
    ##### explore fetchall() results: 2- loop through result and accessing columns by index
    #############################################################
    print('\n2- loop through result and accessing columns by index...')

    for row in rows:
        print(f'[type of row: {type(row)}] {row[0]}, \t {row[1]}')


    #############################################################
    ##### explore fetchall() results: 3- loop through result and accessing columns by name
    #############################################################
    print('\n3- loop through result and accessing columns by name...')

    for row in rows:
        print(f"[type of row: {type(row)}] {row.name}, \t {row.aliased_name},
{row.__getattribute__('spaced name')}")


    #############################################################
    ##### explore cursor description: 4- type of description, see it and get column names
    #############################################################
    print(f'\n4- type of cursor description and print description...')

    print(f'type of cursor description: {type(_cursor.description)}')
    print(_cursor.description)

    ### prepare list of columns of the cursor result by fetchall()
    columns = [col[0] for col in _cursor.description]
    print(columns)
```

```python
    ### print rows
    for row in rows:
        print(row)
    print()


    ################################################################
    ##### explore fetchall() results: 5- convert to pandas dataframe
    ################################################################
    print(f'\n5- convert to pandas dataframe...')
    results = []
    for row in rows:
        results.append(dict(zip(columns, row)))

    df = pd.DataFrame(results)
    print(df)

    ### commit the command if required
    # _connection.commit()

    ### then close the cursor and connection
    _cursor.close()
    _connection.close()

except Exception as ex:
    print(f'ERROR: \n{ex}')
```

For this section 5.1, we are using the following select statement,

```python
sql = "SELECT name, name AS aliased_name, name AS [spaced name] FROM sys.databases;"
```

From the table 'sys.databases', we are reading the all records and we have chosen the following columns

- name: the name of the database
- aliased_name: the name of the database which is aliased as 'aliased_name'
- [spaced name]: the name of the database which is aliased as '[spaced name]' with the space

Then executes the select statement using execute() method of the cursor as

```python
_cursor.execute(sql)
```

And then we will try to get the results from the cursor, the fetchall() is used here as we are sure with the select SQL query that it will have one or more rows, however there are other methods to get the results from the cursor and here we are using fetchall() method.

```
rows = _cursor.fetchall()
```

explore fetchall() results: 1- type of result and print result

In this topic we will see the type of the result that we got from fetchall() method into rows variable. We can check the type or rows using the standard method type() in python as

```
print('\n1- type of result and print rows...')
print(f'type of result: {type(rows)}')
print(rows)
```

explore fetchall() results: 2- loop through result and accessing columns by index

Now we have fetched all the results into rows variable and want to process them further, there is one of the ways to process them using iteration of the rows and accessing the columns by the index of the current row.

```
for row in rows:
    print(f'[type of row: {type(row)}] {row[0]}, \t {row[1]}')
```

The loop is applied on the rows and current record is a row and the 1st and 2nd column are accessed by the index 0 and 1. So the column index starts from 0 (zero).

It will loop through all the rows and the first two column values are printed.

explore fetchall() results: 3- loop through result and accessing columns by name

While looping through the results of the fetchall() method, we can access the columns by the column name also. These column names are those we mentioned in the select SQL statement.

Remember the column names mentioned in the select statement are,

- name: the name of the database
- aliased_name: the name of the database which is aliased as 'aliased_name'
- [spaced name]: the name of the database which is aliased as '[spaced name]' with the space

We can access the columns in the loop as,

```python
for row in rows:
    print(f"[type of row: {type(row)}] {row.name}, \t {row.aliased_name},
{row.__getattribute__('spaced name')}")
```

Notice, that the column names are the properties or the attributes of the row.
The column name without any space can be accessed as the row property. While the column names with the space are accessed using the __getattribute__() method of row.

explore cursor description: 4- type of description, see it and get column names

You may be wondering about the row and column names, how they are being available in the row? Right, so we have seen the type of the rows, and if you iterate over the rows, you can check the type of the current row. It is a specific object in pyodbc which is referenced from the cursor and its method as results.

There is one more object of our interest that is 'description', it is the property of the cursor which has the information regarding the results that is column information.

You can access it and check the type of this object and can explore further,

```python
print(f'type of cursor description: {type(_cursor.description)}')
print(_cursor.description)
```

When you check the type of the description, you will see that it is a list of an object and so you can iterate it.

The interesting part is that most of the time we will be more interested in the column names so we can get the column names as, and the print the rows also,

```python
### prepare list of columns of the cursor result by fetchall()
columns = [col[0] for col in _cursor.description]
print(columns)


### print rows
for row in rows:
    print(row)
print()
```

explore fetchall() results: 5- convert to pandas dataframe

Well, these recipes are designed for Data Engineers/Analysts/Scientist, and they are more interested in the data sets in the form of pandas dataframe.

So we can convert the results of fetchall() method into pandas dataframe. There are different ways to convert the results into pandas dataframe, here is one of the ways to make it work,

```python
    results = []
    for row in rows:
        results.append(dict(zip(columns, row)))


    df = pd.DataFrame(results)
    print(df)
```

In above code block, we are declaring an empty list and the looping through the rows (which is the result of fetchall() method) and converting into dictionary and appending to the list which is finally used to create the pandas dataframe.

5.2. Reading/Selecting data from SQL Database table and exploring fetchval() function

In this recipe, we will discuss about the fetchval() method of the cursor.

Here we will discuss the following topics,

✓ explore fetchval() results: get scalar result from query

pyodbc_05_02_select_fetchval.py

```python
import pyodbc
import pandas as pd
import __connection_string_utils as csutils


# ### prepare/get the connection string
connection_string = csutils.get_odbc_connection_string()


print('connect to sql and select/read data ...\n')


_connection = None
_cursor = None
```

```python
try:
    ### create connection and cursor, and set autocommit to False
    _connection = pyodbc.connect(connection_string)
    _connection.autocommit = False
    _cursor = _connection.cursor()


    #############################################################
    ##### explore fetchval() results: get scalar result from query
    ##### getting scalar value, i.e first row & first column value
    #############################################################


    ### execute the sql commands here
    query = """SELECT COUNT(1) AS total_cutomers, SUM(ID) AS id_sum
                    FROM dbo.customers_tbd
                    WHERE customer_country = ?;"""


    country = 'singapore'
    _cursor.execute(query, country)


    scalar_value = _cursor.fetchval()
    print(f'scalar_value i.e customer counts: {scalar_value}')


    #############################################################
    ##### fetchall() : to get the results from cursor
    # we can use the fetchall() for this scalar resulting query,
    # but we have a dedicated function fetchval(), and we should use it
    #############################################################
    # rows = _cursor.fetchall()
    # print(rows)


    ### commit the command if required
    # _connection.commit()


    ### then close the cursor and connection
    _cursor.close()
    _connection.close()

except Exception as ex:
    print(f'ERROR: {ex}')
```

explore fetchval() results: get scalar result from query

Let say we have a SQL select statement and it returns a single result, this is also called as scalar result and we want to get it and use it further.

Refer the below SQL select statement,

```
query = """SELECT COUNT(1) AS total_cutomers, SUM(ID) AS id_sum
                FROM dbo.customers_tbd
                WHERE customer_country = ?;"""
```

In this query the value of the 'total_customers' column is the scalar result, however in this query there are two resulting columns and will be zero or one row in the results.

So, we want to get the scalar value which is 'total_customers' column value of first row.

This SQL query is also having a placeholder for a parameter, we can execute this query as,

```
country = 'singapore'
_cursor.execute(query, country)
```

To get the scalar result, the cursor have a dedicated method fetchval() and we should use it. However fetchall() method can be used and we have to get the required value by accessing the column name. The later approach can be erroneous if not implemented properly so we must use fetchval() method.

```
scalar_value = _cursor.fetchval()
print(f'scalar_value i.e customer counts: {scalar_value}')
```

Furthermore, on scalar results, the scalar result is the result of the first row and first column.

5.3. Reading/Selecting data from SQL Database table and exploring fetchone() function

In this recipe, we will discuss about fetchone() method of the cursor.

This method fetchone() is used to work with one row at a time.

There may be different scenarios to use this method, here we will see the following 2 scenarios,

- ✓ explore fetchone(): 1- row by row processing with one or more columns
- ✓ explore fetchone(): 2- processing only first row of result set with one or more columns

The code of this recipe is shown below,

```python
import pyodbc
import pandas as pd
import __connection_string_utils as csutils

# ### prepare/get the connection string
connection_string = csutils.get_odbc_connection_string()

print('connect to sql and select/read data ...\n')

_connection = None
_cursor = None
try:
    ### create connection and cursor, and set autocommit to False
    _connection = pyodbc.connect(connection_string)
    _connection.autocommit = False
    _cursor = _connection.cursor()

    ### execute the sql commands here

    ###############################################################
    ##### explore fetchone(): 1- row by row processing with one or more columns
    ##### that is one row at a time
    ###############################################################

    query = """SELECT customer_country, COUNT(1) AS total_customers, SUM(ID) AS id_sum
                FROM dbo.customers_tbd
                GROUP BY customer_country;"""

    _cursor.execute(query)

    print(f'\n1- row by row processing with one or more columns...')
    while True:
        row = _cursor.fetchone()

        if not row:
            print('no more rows')
            break

        print(f'row by row processing with one or more columns, counts: {row.total_customers},
or sum: {row[1]}')
```

```python
    ################################################################
    ##### explore fetchone(): 2- processing only first row of result set with one or more
columns
    ##### that is only first row
    ################################################################

    ### another use case is this
    query = """SELECT customer_country, COUNT(1) AS total_customers, SUM(ID) AS id_sum
                FROM dbo.customers_tbd
                GROUP BY customer_country;"""

    _cursor.execute(query)


    print(f'\n2- processing only first row of result set with one or more columns...')

    row = _cursor.fetchone()

    counts = row.total_customers
    sum = row[1]
    print(f'counts: {counts}')
    print(f'sum: {sum}')


    ### commit the command if required
    # _connection.commit()

    ### then close the cursor and connection
    _cursor.close()
    _connection.close()

except Exception as ex:
    print(f'could not connect\n{ex}')
```

explore fetchone(): 1- row by row processing with one or more columns

When we want to process a row at a time, we can use the fetcone() method.

We are using the following SQL select statement,

```python
    query = """SELECT customer_country, COUNT(1) AS total_customers, SUM(ID) AS id_sum
                FROM dbo.customers_tbd
                GROUP BY customer_country;"""
```

It is an aggregation query which outputs customer_country, to_customers, and id_sum for each customer_country for example.

We can execute this query as,

```
_cursor.execute(query)
```

Then we can use the while loop of python to process a row at a time using fetchone() method of the cursor.

The while loop must be implemented properly to handle the situation when there is no further result or row, in this case the loop must be exited.

Also, we can access the desired columns as required.

```
while True:
    row = _cursor.fetchone()

    if not row:
        print('no more rows')
        break

    print(f'row by row processing with one or more columns, counts: {row.total_customers},
or sum: {row[1]}')
```

Notice the last print statement in which we are accessing columns by index as well by name.

explore fetchone(): 2- processing only first row of result set with one or more columns

In this scenario, we are interested in the only first row of result and its column values.

The following is the SQL select statement which is executed and then we access the first row and its column values as,

```
query = """SELECT customer_country, COUNT(1) AS total_customers, SUM(ID) AS id_sum
            FROM dbo.customers_tbd
            GROUP BY customer_country;"""
_cursor.execute(query)
```

```python
print(f'\n2- processing only first row of result set with one or more columns...')

row = _cursor.fetchone()

counts = row.total_customers
sum = row[1]
print(f'counts: {counts}')
print(f'sum: {sum}')
```

Notice, that we are accessing the columns by name and index here.

5.4. Reading/Selecting data from SQL Database table and exploring fetchmany() function

There is one more method fetchmany() of the cursor which is used when we want to process the records or rows in a batch. This batch can be specified in terms of the number of rows.

pyodbc_05_04_select_fetchmany.py

```python
import pyodbc
import pandas as pd
import __connection_string_utils as csutils

# ### prepare/get the connection string
connection_string = csutils.get_odbc_connection_string()

print('connect to sql and select/read data ...\n')

_connection = None
_cursor = None
try:
    ### create connection and cursor, and set autocommit to False
    _connection = pyodbc.connect(connection_string)
    _connection.autocommit = False
    _cursor = _connection.cursor()

    ### execute the sql commands here

    ################################################################
    ##### explore fetchone(): 1- row by row processing in a batch
    ##### that is multiple rows at a time
    ################################################################
```

```python
    query = """SELECT * FROM sys.tables;"""


    _cursor.execute(query)


    print(f'\n1- row by row processing in a batch...')
    batch = 1
    while True:
        rows = _cursor.fetchmany(10)

        if not rows:
            print('no more rows')
            break


        for row in rows:
            print(f'batch: {batch} - row by row processing in a batch, tablename: {row.name},
or \t object_id: {row[1]}')


        batch = batch + 1


    ### commit the command if required
    _connection.commit()


    ### then close the cursor and connection
    _cursor.close()
    _connection.close()

except Exception as ex:
    print(f'could not connect\n{ex}')
```

explore fetchmany(): 1- row by row processing in a batch

Let say we have a SQL select statement,

```python
    query = """SELECT * FROM sys.tables;"""
```

We can execute it,

```python
    _cursor.execute(query)
```

Then write while loop to process the records in a batch of 10 rows at a time, the while loop must handle the case when there are no records to process.

The batch of records or rows is iterated using the for loop and we can access the required columns by either index or by column name as,

```python
batch = 1
while True:
    rows = _cursor.fetchmany(10)

    if not rows:
        print('no more rows')
        break

    for row in rows:
        print(f'batch: {batch} - row by row processing in a batch, tablename: {row.name},
or \t object_id: {row[1]}')

    batch = batch + 1
```

Notice, the variable batch is initialized with the value 1 and it is incremented inside while loop, so using the variable batch we can determine the number of batches.

Also, in case of no records the while loop is exited using break statement.

Then the records in the batch are iterated using for loop and columns are accessed by index as well column name to process it further.

6.0. Reading/Selecting data from SQL Database table using read_sql(), read_sql_query() of pandas

In this recipe we will explore the two of the methods of pandas to query or read the data from the SQL database table.

These are the two scenarios,

✓ pandas.read_sql(): 1- execute sql query and get result in pandas dataframe
✓ pandas.read_sql_query(): 2- execute sql query and get result in pandas dataframe

pyodbc_06_select_pd.py

```python
import pyodbc
import pandas as pd
```

```python
import __connection_string_utils as csutils

# ### prepare/get the connection string
connection_string = csutils.get_odbc_connection_string()

print('connect to sql and select/read data ...\n')

_connection = None
_cursor = None
try:
    ### create connection and cursor, and set autocommit to False
    _connection = pyodbc.connect(connection_string)
    _connection.autocommit = False
    _cursor = _connection.cursor()

    ### execute the sql commands here

    ##################################################################
    ##### pandas.read_sql(): 1- execute sql query and get result in pandas dataframe
    ##### pandas.read_sql_query(): 2- execute sql query and get result in pandas dataframe
    ##################################################################

    query = 'SELECT * FROM sys.tables;'

    print(f'\npandas.read_sql(): 1- execute sql query and get result in pandas dataframe...')
    df_pd = pd.read_sql(query, _connection)
    print(df_pd)

    print(f'\npandas.read_sql_query(): 2- execute sql query and get result in pandas dataframe...')
    another_df = pd.read_sql_query(query, _connection)
    print(another_df)

    ### commit the command if required
    # _connection.commit()

    ### then close the connection
    _connection.close()

except Exception as ex:
    print(f'could not connect\n{ex}')
```

pandas.read_sql(): 1- execute sql query and get result in pandas dataframe

Pandas has a method named read_sql(), it is used to read the data from the SQL database table. This method is the wrapper of two other methods read_sql_table() and read_sql_query().

The read_sql_table(), as name hints it is used to read a sql table.
The read_sql_query(), as name hints it is used to read the data using SQL query.

So, based on the inputs to the read_sql() method, it calls the corresponding method and return the result in a pandas dataframe.

When you have a SQL select query to read the data, we can use either read_sql() method or read_sql_query() method.

It is simple as,

```
query = 'SELECT * FROM sys.tables;'


print(f'\npandas.read_sql(): 1- execute sql query and get result in pandas dataframe...')
df_pd = pd.read_sql(query, _connection)
print(df_pd)
```

Notice, in the method read_sql_query(), the SQL statement is the first parameter and _connection is the second parameter. The _connection is the pyodbc sql connection created using pyodbc.connect() method with connection string.

pandas.read_sql_query(): 2- execute sql query and get result in pandas dataframe

As described just above, read_sql-query() is dedicated method to read data using SQL query.

It is simple as,

```
query = 'SELECT * FROM sys.tables;'

print(f'\npandas.read_sql_query(): 2- execute sql query and get result in pandas
dataframe...')
another_df = pd.read_sql_query(query, _connection)
print(another_df)
```

Notice, in the method read_sql_query(), the SQL statement is the first parameter and _connection is the second parameter. The _connection is the pyodbc sql connection created using pyodbc.connect() method with connection string.

7.0. Executing/calling user stored procedures (USP) and exploring nextset()

In this recipe we will discuss about executing the User defined Stored Procedures (USP) in SQL.

Most of the times we have very complex business logic wrapped in an USP to read the data after applying some business logic.

This is not mandatory that the USP must be complex, it could be as simple as a select statement also.

Here we will look at the following scenarios,

- ✓ execute usp: 1- calling usp without parameters & returns a resultset
- ✓ execute usp: 2- calling usp with parameters that returns scalar value
- ✓ execute usp: 3- calling usp with parameters, rows affected
- ✓ execute usp: 4- calling usp with parameters & multiple resultset
- ✓ execute usp: 5- calling usp in a loop multiple times
- ✓ execute usp: 6- calling usp with OUTPUT parameter

pyodbc_07_usp.py

```python
import pyodbc
import pandas as pd
import __connection_string_utils as csutils


# ### prepare/get the connection string
connection_string = csutils.get_odbc_connection_string()


print('connect to sql and execute stored procedures ...\n')


_connection = None
_cursor = None
try:
    ### create connection and cursor, and set autocommit to False
    _connection = pyodbc.connect(connection_string)
    _connection.autocommit = False
    _cursor = _connection.cursor()

    ### execute the sql commands here
    ################################################################
    ##### execute usp: 1- calling usp without parameters & returns a resultset
    ################################################################
    ### 1
    sql = '''EXECUTE dbo.usp_getdata_tbd'''
```

```python
_cursor.execute(sql)
result = _cursor.fetchall()

print(f'\n1-calling usp without parameters & returns a resultset...')
print(result)


##################################################################
##### execute usp: 2- calling usp with parameters that returns scalar value
##################################################################

# both syntax works
sql = '''{call dbo.usp_insert_tbd (?, ?, ?)}'''

sql = """
    EXEC dbo.usp_insert_tbd @customer_name = ?, @customer_country = ?, @is_b2b_customer =
?
    """
params = ('customer name', 'customer country', True)

_cursor.execute(sql, params)
last_id = int(_cursor.fetchval())
_cursor.commit()

print(f'\n2- calling usp with parameters that returns scalar value...')
print(f'last_id: {last_id}')


##################################################################
##### execute usp: 3- calling usp with parameters, rows affected
##################################################################
### 3
sql = "{call [dbo].[usp_update_tbd] (?, ?)}"

id = 11
params = (id, 'NEW CUSTOMER NAME')

_cursor.execute(sql, params)
result = _cursor.rowcount

print(f'\n3- calling usp with parameters, rows affected...')
print(f'rows affected: {result}')


##################################################################
##### execute usp: 4- calling usp with parameters & multiple resultset
##################################################################
### 4
```

```python
sql = '{call [dbo].[usp_getdata_by_country_tbd](?)}'

params = ('singapore')

_cursor.execute(sql, params)

print(f'\n4- calling usp with parameters & multiple resultset...')
counter = 1

resultset = _cursor.fetchall()

print(f'result set: {counter}')
print(resultset)

while True:
    if _cursor.nextset():
        resultset = _cursor.fetchall()

        counter = counter + 1
        print(f'result set: {counter}')
        print(resultset)
    else:
        break


###################################################################
##### execute usp: 5- calling usp in a loop multiple times
###################################################################
### 5
print('5. call dbo.usp_insert_tbd :')
data = {'custname': ['rajesh', 'sunil', 'priyanka'],
        'country': ['India', 'India', 'Singapore'],
        'isb2b':[True, True, False],
        'currency':['indian rupee', 'indian rupee', 'singapore dollar']}

df = pd.DataFrame(data)

records_df = df[['custname', 'country', 'isb2b']]
print(records_df)

params = [tuple(row) for ix, row in records_df.iterrows()]

sql = '{call dbo.usp_insert_tbd (?, ?, ?)}'

id_list = []
for param in params:
```

```python
        _cursor.execute(sql, param)
        curr_id = int(_cursor.fetchval())

        id_list.append(curr_id)
        _cursor.commit()

    print(f'\n5- calling usp in a loop multiple times...')
    print(f'ids of inserted records: {id_list}')


    ################################################################
    ##### execute usp: 6- calling usp with OUTPUT parameter
    ################################################################
    ### 6
    sql = '''DECLARE @output_param INT
        EXECUTE dbo.usp_getcounts_tbd @output_param OUTPUT;
        SELECT @output_param AS record_counts;'''

    _cursor.execute(sql)

    result = _cursor.fetchval()

    print(f'\n6- calling usp with OUTPUT parameter...')
    print(f'result: {result}')


    ### commit the command if required
    _connection.commit()

    ### then close the cursor and connection
    _cursor.close()
    _connection.close()

except Exception as ex:
    print(f'could not connect\n{ex}')
```

execute usp: 1- calling usp without parameters & returns a resultset

Let say we have a USP that does not need any parameters and returns a result set, we can execute it as,

```python
    sql = '''EXECUTE dbo.usp_getdata_tbd'''

    _cursor.execute(sql)
    result = _cursor.fetchall()
```

```
print(f'\n1-calling usp without parameters & returns a resultset...')
print(result)
```

Notice, the USP "dbo.usp_getdata_tbd" is mentioned in a string variable sql with EXECUTE SQL keyword and within 3 single quotes as,

```
sql = '''EXECUTE dbo.usp_getdata_tbd'''
```

The results of the USP are taken into result variable using fetchall() method of the cursor and this result can be processed further.

execute usp: 2- calling usp with parameters that returns scalar value

In this recipe we will discuss about executing an USP with parameters that returns a scalar value.

The user stored procedure (USP) in SQL may have several input parameters and may return a scalar value.

In this example the USP 'dbo.usp_insert_tbd' takes 3 parameters and returns the identity (id) value of the inserted record.

We can execute this USP using 'call' keyword in pyodbc or EXEC (execute) keyword in TSQL, these both way works fine.

The parameters are passed using the question mark (?) place holder. The tuple of parameter is prepared and passed to execute() method of the cursor.

```
sql = '''{call dbo.usp_insert_tbd (?, ?, ?)}'''

sql = """
    EXEC dbo.usp_insert_tbd @customer_name = ?, @customer_country = ?, @is_b2b_customer =
?
    """
params = ('customer name', 'customer country', True)


_cursor.execute(sql, params)
last_id = int(_cursor.fetchval())
_cursor.commit()


print(f'\n2- calling usp with parameters that returns scalar value...')
print(f'last_id: {last_id}')
```

Notice, that fetchval() method of cursor is used to get the scalar value, in this example we are sure that this scalar value will be integer and hence we are casting it to the integer using int() in python.

As we inserting a record in the database table so do not forget to commit the operation, we have committed it using commit() method of the cursor and (as well connection at last), sometimes in different pyodbc versions the cursor.commit() does not behaves as expected so make sure that connection.commit() is used at last to commit the transaction carried out by cursor.

execute usp: 3- calling usp with parameters, rows affected

In this recipe, we will discuss about executing an USP that takes parameters. An USP may affect the rows in the database table, and we want to get how many rows were affected.

We have an USP 'dbo.usp_update_tbd', this USP takes 2 parameters, the 'id', and 'customer_name'. It updates records in the database table and modifies the customer name with the new name of the customer where the ID column matches the input id value.

The parameters are passed as a tuple into the execute() method of cursor, and then 'rowcount' property is used to get the number of rows affected by this USP.

```python
sql = "{call [dbo].[usp_update_tbd] (?, ?)}"

id = 11
params = (id, 'NEW CUSTOMER NAME')

_cursor.execute(sql, params)
result = _cursor.rowcount

print(f'\n3- calling usp with parameters, rows affected...')
print(f'rows affected: {result}')
```

Notice, the 'call' keyword is used to prepare the USP execution SQL, and the schema in the database i.e. dbo and the USP name can be wrapped within square brackets ([]) separated by a dot (.).

execute usp: 4- calling usp with parameters & multiple resultset

In this recipe, we will discuss about executing an USP with parameters and that may return multiple result sets.

Let say we an USP 'usp_getdata_by_country_tbd' that takes one parameter 'the name of the country' and returns multiple result sets at least 2 in this example.

We can simply execute this USP using execute() of the cursor.

Then, we should use fetchall() or fetchval() method to get the first result set whichever is possible as per USP and then we should use the 'while' loop to get further result sets and it must be implemented to handle the case when there is no more result set.

The call to this USP is made as,

```python
sql = '{call [dbo].[usp_getdata_by_country_tbd](?)}'


params = ('singapore')


_cursor.execute(sql, params)


print(f'\n4- calling usp with parameters & multiple resultset...')
counter = 1


resultset = _cursor.fetchall()


print(f'result set: {counter}')
print(resultset)


while True:
    if _cursor.nextset():
        resultset = _cursor.fetchall()

        counter = counter + 1
        print(f'result set: {counter}')
        print(resultset)
    else:
        break
```

Notice, the first result set is taken just above the while loop and then further results are handled in the while loop, to check if there is next result set, the nextset() of the cursor is used and fetchall() method is used to take the results.

If there is no result set in the loop, the loop is exited using the break.

execute usp: 5- calling usp in a loop multiple times

In this recipe, we will discuss about an USP with parameters that is executed multiple times using a loop for different set of parameters.

Let say we have an USP 'dbo.usp_insert_tbd' that inserts a row into the database table, and it takes 3 parameters.

We have a dataframe with multiple rows and these must be inserted into the database table, the following 3 columns are used to pass the parameters to the USP,

- custname
- country
- isb2b

The list of tuples is prepared to create parameters using python comprehension, the params is the variable that is list of tuples.

And the SQL to call an USP is prepared with 'call' keyword and parameters are marked as place holder symbol question mark (?) as,

```python
data = {'custname': ['rajesh', 'sunil', 'priyanka'],
        'country': ['India', 'India', 'Singapore'],
        'isb2b':[True, True, False],
        'currency':['indian rupee', 'indian rupee', 'singapore dollar']}


df = pd.DataFrame(data)


records_df = df[['custname', 'country', 'isb2b']]
print(records_df)


params = [tuple(row) for ix, row in records_df.iterrows()]


sql = '{call dbo.usp_insert_tbd (?, ?, ?)}'
```

Then the for loop is used to execute the USP for each tuple which represents a row in the dataframe,

```python
id_list = []
for param in params:
    _cursor.execute(sql, param)
    curr_id = int(_cursor.fetchval())

    id_list.append(curr_id)
    _cursor.commit()

print(f'\n5- calling usp in a loop multiple times...')
print(f'ids of inserted records: {id_list}')
```

The USP is executed using the execute() method of the cursor and param is passed within the loop. The fetchval() method is used to get the id of the inserted record which is appended to the id_list list in python.

Notice, by using the commit() method of cursor and (as well connection at last), sometimes in different pyodbc versions the cursor.commit() does not behaves as expected so make sure that connection.commit() is used at last to commit the transaction carried out by cursor.

execute usp: 6- calling usp with OUTPUT parameter

In this recipe, we will discuss about executing an USP that that return the value using OUTPUT parameter in SQL.

There are different ways to call an USP with output parameters, and the simplest way is the SQL approach. IN SQL such an USP is called using EXECUTE keyword and by declaring the parameters and marking as OUTPUT.

In this example we have an USP 'dbo.usp_getcounts', which takes one parameter as output, we have declared the variable '@output_param' which is of type SQL INT, and EXECUTE keyword makes the call to the usp and that variable is marked as OUTPUT and then a SELECT statement is used to get the value.

```
sql = '''DECLARE @output_param INT
    EXECUTE dbo.usp_getcounts_tbd @output_param OUTPUT;
    SELECT @output_param AS record_counts;'''


_cursor.execute(sql)


result = _cursor.fetchval()


print(f'\n6- calling usp with OUTPUT parameter...')
print(f'result: {result}')
```

NOTES:
Sometimes in different pyodbc versions the cursor.commit() does not behaves as expected so make sure that connection.commit() is used at last to commit the transaction performed by the cursor.

8.0. Executing SQL query in multiple databases using loop

In this recipe we will discuss how we can execute SQL query in multiple databases.

There may be a scenario where we have a SQL query and want to execute in a list of databases (multiple databases). This SQL query can be to create a table, to perform a DDL operation, or to perform a DCL operation, or even as simple as DML operation.

Most of the time, table, USP creation or deployment in multiple databases or deleting a table from multiple databases is the best scenario.

Here we will look at the following scenarios,

- ✓ loop through databases: executing sql query in multiple databases

```python
import pyodbc
import __connection_string_utils as csutils
import __connection_details_sqlserver as sqldetails


# ### prepare/get the connection string
connection_string = csutils.get_odbc_connection_string()


############################################################
##### loop through databases: executing sql query in multiple databases
############################################################


print('connect to sql and execute query ...\n')


list_dbs = ['db-customer1', 'db-customer2']


for db in list_dbs:
    print(f'db: {db}')

    ### ### read details
    if 1 == 1:
        ### at least the following details
        DRIVER = sqldetails.DRIVER
        SERVER = sqldetails.SERVER
        DATABASE = db #sqldetails.DATABASE
        USERID = sqldetails.USERID
        PASSWORD = sqldetails.PASSWORD
        ### additional details
        ENCRYPT = sqldetails.ENCRYPT
        TRUSTSERVERCERTIFICATE = sqldetails.TRUSTSERVERCERTIFICATE
        CONNECTION_TIMEOUT = sqldetails.CONNECTION_TIMEOUT
        PACKET_SIZE = sqldetails.PACKET_SIZE
```

69

```python
### prepare connection string here
connection_string = f'''Driver={DRIVER};
Server={SERVER};
Database={DATABASE};
Uid={USERID};
Pwd={PASSWORD};
Encrypt=yes;
TrustServerCertificate=no;
Connection Timeout=1800;
Packet Size=4096;'''


_connection = None
_cursor = None
try:
    ### create connection and cursor, and set autocommit to False
    _connection = pyodbc.connect(connection_string)
    _connection.autocommit = False
    _cursor = _connection.cursor()


    ### execute the sql commands here

    ################################################################
    ##### any sql command that you want to execute in the listed multiple databases
    ##### such as creating a table in all databases or deleting a table from all databases
    ##### or shrinking the log file in all the databases, and so on
    ################################################################

    sql = """CREATE TABLE dbo.currencies_tbd(
        ID INT IDENTITY(1, 1),
        currency NVARCHAR(20) NOT NULL,
        currency_description NVARCHAR(20) NOT NULL,
    )"""

    _cursor.execute(sql)
    print('sql command executed')

    ### commit the command if required
    _connection.commit()

    ### then close the cursor and connection
    _cursor.close()
    _connection.close()

except Exception as ex:
    print(f'could not connect sql server & execute sql query\n{ex}')
```

loop through databases: executing sql query in multiple databases

Here we have a list of databases,

```
list_dbs = ['db-customer-1-dev', 'db-customer-2-dev', 'db-customer-3-dev']
```

We have a SQL statement to create a table as,

```
sql = """CREATE TABLE dbo.currencies_tbd(
    ID INT IDENTITY(1, 1),
    currency NVARCHAR(20) NOT NULL,
    currency_description NVARCHAR(20) NOT NULL,
)"""
```

We want to create this table in multiple databases mentioned in the list_dbs list.

So, we must loop through the list of databases, and we will get the current database, then we need to create or prepare the SQL connection string and connect to the current SQL Server, and then execute the SQL statement to create the table in the current database.

This will be iterated over the list of all databases.

Notice, create table statement will change the state of the database and hence we must commit the transaction performed by using connection.commit() method.

NOTES:
See the import statements in this recipe, they are explained in the starting and I hope you went through this if not please read it from start of the book.

These were few of the scenarios to work with Microsoft SQL Server in Python using PYODBC library. These recipes are enough to implement your database related tasks in Data Engineer, Analyst, and Scientist profile. They are very helpful recipes for data folks even they are only Application developers.

SQLALCHEMY Code recipes

Preparing SQL server connection string

To prepare the SQL server connection string read the following topics above.

- Making connection string
- How to avoid creating connection string every time?

1.   Making connection to SQL Server – 2 ways

1.1.   making connection to SQL Server

There are the following approaches or ways to connect SQL Server database,

approach: 1 - using 'with' statement using engine_url() and create_engine()

Using SQLALCHEMY library we can create the connection to the SQL Server. There are many approaches or ways to create the connection.

Here is one of the ways to create SQL Server connection using the SQL Connection String and the sqlalchemy engine url,

sqlalchemy_01_01_making_connection.py

```python
import sqlalchemy as sa
import __connection_string_utils as csutils


connection_string = csutils.get_odbc_connection_string()


print('connecting to sql ...\n')
##################################################################
##### approach: 1 - using 'with' statement using engine url and create_engine()
##################################################################
# using ''with' the connection is automatically closed when leaving the 'with' block

try:
    ### create engine url and the engine
    engine_url = sa.engine.URL.create("mssql+pyodbc", query = dict(odbc_connect =
connection_string))
    engine = sa.create_engine(engine_url, fast_executemany = True)

    ### create a connection and execute the sql
    ### it automatically closes the connection
```

```python
with engine.connect() as connection:
    try:
        if not connection.closed:
            print('connected successfully')
            print(f'Is connection closed? : {connection.closed}')


        ### execute the sql query here
    except Exception as ex:
        print(f'\terror: \n{str(ex)}')


    print(f'Is connection closed? : {connection.closed}')


except Exception as ex:
    print(f'could not connect\n{ex}')
```

Here the following line is an import statement which is importing a custom module that we created in start of the book (kindly read that topic above in starting), this module has method which return the SQL connection string.

```python
import __connection_string_utils as csutils


connection_string = csutils.get_odbc_connection_string()
```

Then we are creating an engine URL using connection string which is ODBC connection string as,

```python
engine_url = sa.engine.URL.create("mssql+pyodbc", query = dict(odbc_connect = connection_string))
```

After creating engine URL, we need to create an engine using engine_url as,

```python
engine = sa.create_engine(engine_url, fast_executemany = True)
```

Notice, fast_executemany = True, this is an option to enable the fast operation execution and enabling many operations execution. We must keep it enabled while working with SQL Server database.

It helps to increase SQL server operations execution for reading the data from database tables or inserting the data into database tables. When this is enabled, SQLALCHEMY optimizes its code to handle the command execution with increased performance internally.

Once we have created the engine, we can create the connection using engine.connect() method and it returns the connection object. Here we are using the 'with' statement so that the connection is handled by 'with' statement when it reaches the end of the code block. It automatically closes the connection.

```python
with engine.connect() as connection:
    try:
        if not connection.closed:
            print('connected successfully')
            print(f'Is connection closed? : {connection.closed}')


        ### execute the sql query here
    except Exception as ex:
        print(f'\terror: \n{str(ex)}')
```

Notice, connection has a property named as 'closed', which gives the status of the connection whether it is connected or not using True/False values.

After making connection, the SQL commands/queries/statements can be executed, then it goes out of the 'with' code block and the connection is closed, we can check it again out of 'with' code block as,

```python
print(f'Is connection closed? : {connection.closed}')
```

This is one of the way we can create a SQL Server connection using engine URL and the engine.connect() method of SQLALCHEMY.

The SQL commands/statements or queries may or may not changes the database state, and hence in case it is changing the state of the database than that transaction or operation should be committed to reflect the changes made such as updating, deleting rows, creating, and deleting the table, USP, functions etc.

So, how we can handle the transaction commit we will see whenever they are used in next recipes.

1.2.   making connection to SQL Server another way

Using SQLALCHEMY library we can create the connection to the SQL Server. There are many approaches or ways to create the connection.

Here is another way to create SQL Server connection using the SQL Connection String and the quote_plus() and the sqlalchemy create_engine() and engine.connect() method,

approach: 1 - using 'with' statement using quote_plus() and create_engine()

```python
import sqlalchemy as sa
from urllib.parse import quote_plus
import __connection_string_utils as csutils


connection_string = csutils.get_odbc_connection_string()


print('connecting to sql ...\n')
################################################################
##### approach: 1 - using 'with' statement using quote_plus() and create_engine()
################################################################
# using ''with' the connection is automatically closed when leaving the 'with' block

try:
    ### create engine url and the engine

    quoted = quote_plus(connection_string)
    engine = sa.create_engine('mssql+pyodbc:///?odbc_connect={}'.format(quoted))


    ### create a connection and execute the sql
    ### it automatically closes the connection
    with engine.connect() as connection:
        try:
            if not connection.closed:
                print('connected successfully')
                print(f'Is connection closed? : {connection.closed}')


            ### execute the sql query here
        except Exception as ex:
            print(f'\terror: \n{str(ex)}')

    print(f'Is connection closed? : {connection.closed}')

except Exception as ex:
    print(f'could not connect\n{ex}')
```

In this approach, we using quote_plus() method of urllib.parse library, which handles the quotes in the sql connection string particularly here and return a string object as,

```python
quoted = quote_plus(connection_string)
```

Then the SQLALCHEMY engine is created as,

```
engine = sa.create_engine('mssql+pyodbc:///?odbc_connect={}'.format(quoted))
```

After creating engine, we can connect the SQL Server database using engine.connect() method which return a connection object.

Again, we are using the 'with' statement and it handles the closing of connection when it goes out of the scope. Then we can execute any SQL statement or command here as,

```
with engine.connect() as connection:
    try:
        if not connection.closed:
            print('connected successfully')
            print(f'Is connection closed? : {connection.closed}')


        ### execute the sql query here
    except Exception as ex:
        print(f'\terror: \n{str(ex)}')


print(f'Is connection closed? : {connection.closed}')
```

Notice, the 'closed' property of the connection which gives the status of the connection. After the 'with' statement, we are checking where the connection is closed now or not.

This is another way to connect the SQL Server database.

The SQL commands/statements or queries may or may not changes the database state, and hence in case it is changing the state of the database than that transaction or operation should be committed to reflect the changes made such as updating, deleting rows, creating, and deleting the table, USP, functions etc.

So, how we can handle the transaction commit we will see whenever they are used in next recipes.

2.0. Reading/Selecting data from SQL Database table, using read_sql_table(), read_sql(), read_sql_query() of pandas

In this recipe we will see how we can read or select the data from the database tables using SQLALCHEMY connection and pandas methods.

There are many ways or approaches to read or select or query the data using SQLALCHEMY and pandas, specifically we will discuss the following approaches,

- ✓ approach: 1 - read sql table using pandas
- ✓ approach: 2 - select data by sql without parameters using pandas
- ✓ approach: 3 - select data by sql stored procedure without parameters using pandas
- ✓ approach: 4 - select data by sql with parameters using pandas
- ✓ approach: 5 - select data by sql with parameters (equality and IN) using pandas

`sqlalchemy_02_select_data.py`

```python
import sqlalchemy as sa
from sqlalchemy.sql import text
from sqlalchemy import bindparam
import pandas as pd
import __connection_string_utils as csutils


connection_string = csutils.get_odbc_connection_string()

print('connect to sql and select or read data ...\n')
try:
    ### create engine url and the engine
    engine_url = sa.engine.URL.create("mssql+pyodbc", query = dict(odbc_connect =
connection_string))
    engine = sa.create_engine(engine_url, fast_executemany = True)

    ### create a connection and execute the sql
    ### it automatically closes the connection
    with engine.connect() as connection:
        ### execute the sql query here

        ################################################################
        ##### approach: 1 - read sql table using pandas
        ################################################################

        df = pd.read_sql_table(table_name = 'customers_tbd', schema = 'dbo', con = connection)

        print('\n1 - read sql table using pandas...')
        print(df)


        ################################################################
        ##### approach: 2 - select data by sql without parameters using pandas
        ################################################################
```

```python
query = "SELECT name, name AS aliased_name FROM sys.databases;"

df = pd.read_sql_query(text(query), connection)
# df2 = pd.read_sql(text(query), connection) # SHOULD USE OTHER METHODS
# df3 = pd.read_sql_query(text(query), connection)

print('\n2 - select data by sql without parameters using pandas...')
print(df)


################################################################
##### approach: 3 - select data by sql stored procedure without parameters using
pandas
################################################################

query = '''EXECUTE dbo.usp_getdata_tbd'''
df = pd.read_sql_query(text(query), connection)

print(f'\n3 - select data by sql stored procedure without parameters using pandas...')
print(df)


################################################################
##### approach: 4 - select data by sql with parameters using pandas
################################################################

query = """SELECT COUNT(1) AS total_cutomers, SUM(ID) AS id_sum
    FROM dbo.customers_tbd
    WHERE customer_country = :country"""

params = {'country': 'Singapore'}
df = pd.read_sql_query(text(query), connection, params = params)

print(f'\n4 - select data by sql with parameters using pandas...')
print(df)


################################################################
##### approach: 5 - select data by sql with parameters (equality and IN) using pandas
################################################################

query = """SELECT * FROM dbo.customers_tbd
WHERE customer_country IN :list_countries
AND is_b2b_customer = :isb2b
AND ID IN :ids"""

list_countries = ["India", "Singapore"]
is_b2b = [True]
```

```
    ids = [9, 10, 13, 14, 15]
    params = {'list_countries' : list_countries, 'isb2b' : is_b2b, 'ids' : ids}

    query = text(query)
    query = query.bindparams(
        bindparam('list_countries', expanding = True),
        bindparam('isb2b', expanding = True),
        bindparam('ids', expanding = True),
    )
    df = pd.read_sql_query(query, connection, params=params)

    print(f'\n5 - select data by sql with parameters (equality and IN) using pandas...')
    print(df)

except Exception as ex:
    print(f'ERROR:\n{ex}')
```

Here we are creating a connection to the SQL Database in which we have the tables and data. The connection to SQL database is simple using 'with' statement as described above and then we will read the data with all the approaches mentioned above as,

```
### create engine url and the engine
engine_url = sa.engine.URL.create("mssql+pyodbc", query = dict(odbc_connect =
connection_string))
engine = sa.create_engine(engine_url, fast_executemany = True)

### create a connection and execute the sql
### it automatically closes the connection
with engine.connect() as connection:
    ### execute the sql query here
```

approach: 1 - read sql table using pandas

Let say we have database table, and we want to read all the rows of this table,

```
    df = pd.read_sql_table(table_name = 'customers_tbd', schema = 'dbo', con = connection)

    print('\n1 - read sql table using pandas...')
    print(df)
```

We have used the read_sql_table() method of pandas library where we are passing the table name, schema name and the connection.

approach: 2 - select data by sql without parameters using pandas

Let say we have a simple select statement of SQL to read the data, it may be with or without join of multiple tables, we can simply pass that SQL query and read the data as,

```python
query = "SELECT name, name AS aliased_name FROM sys.databases;"


df = pd.read_sql_query(text(query), connection)
# df2 = pd.read_sql(text(query), connection) # SHOULD USE OTHER METHODS
# df3 = pd.read_sql_query(text(query), connection)

print('\n2 - select data by sql without parameters using pandas...')
print(df)
```

This SQL select query is plain query without any parameters.

As you have noticed, we have used read_sql_query() method of pandas and we are passing the SQL query wrapped within 'text' method of sqlalchemy.sql library.

Actually, pandas provide 3 different methods,

- read_sql_table()
- read_sql_query()
- read_sql()

read_sql_table() method is used to read the table
read_sql_query() method is used to read data using SQL query
read_sql() method is the wrapper of the other 2 methods, and based on the input it calls one of the method. We have details on these 3 methods in another topic above in PYODBC recipes, kindly see it.

approach: 3 - select data by sql stored procedure without parameters using pandas

Let say, we have an SQL user stored procedure (USP) which is used to read data from database tables based on some business logic and it does not need any parameters.

We can read the data using USP without parameters as,

```python
query = '''EXECUTE dbo.usp_getdata_tbd'''
df = pd.read_sql_query(text(query), connection)
```

```
print(f'\n3 - select data by sql stored procedure without parameters using pandas...')
print(df)
```

Notice, we have called an USP that is not taking any input parameters. The SQL call of the USP is prepared and it is passed to the read_sql_query() method along with connection.

approach: 4 - select data by sql with parameters using pandas

In this approach, we will see how we can read the data by a SQL query with parameters.

Let say we have written a SQL query to read the data as shown below. This is taking a parameter named as country, it is marked with the colon (:) parameter name placeholder syntax.

And hence we must pass the required parameters, here only one parameter is required so we have passed it as a dictionary with only key 'country', the only parameter.

```
query = """SELECT COUNT(1) AS total_cutomers, SUM(ID) AS id_sum
    FROM dbo.customers_tbd
    WHERE customer_country = :country"""


params = {'country': 'Singapore'}
df = pd.read_sql_query(text(query), connection, params = params)


print(f'\n4 - select data by sql with parameters using pandas...')
print(df)
```

Notice, the read_sql_query() method of panadas is called and we are passing the SQL query wrapped in text() method, the connection, and the parameter.

approach: 5 - select data by sql with parameters (equality and IN) using pandas

In this approach, we will discuss about reading or selecting the data by a SQL query that takes input parameters.

As you might be aware that in SQL, there is a logical operator called 'IN', that is used to specify multiple values to be checked in a condition. It is possible to have a SQL query with 'IN' operator to read or select the data.

Let say we have the following SQL query,

```
query = """SELECT * FROM dbo.customers_tbd
    WHERE customer_country IN :list_countries
```

```
       AND is_b2b_customer = :isb2b
       AND ID IN :ids"""
```

This SQL query requires 3 parameters marked with placeholders,

:list_countries – It is specified with IN operator
:isb2b – It is specified with to check the equality
:ids - It is specified with IN operator

And we have declared the parameter variables I python as,

```
list_countries = ["India", "Singapore"]
is_b2b = [True]
ids = [9, 10, 13, 14, 15]
params = {'list_countries' : list_countries, 'isb2b' : is_b2b, 'ids' : ids}
```

Now, first we should wrap the SQL query in text() of sqlalchemy.sql and bind the corresponding parameters as,

```
query = text(query)
query = query.bindparams(
    bindparam('list_countries', expanding = True),
    bindparam('isb2b', expanding = True),
    bindparam('ids', expanding = True),
)
df = pd.read_sql_query(query, connection, params=params)

print(f'\n5 - select data by sql with parameters (equality and IN) using pandas...')
print(df)
```

As you noticed, bindparameters() method comes from the SQL query variable which is of type string and wrapped by text() method, the bindparam comes from the sqlalchemy (from sqlalchemy import bindparam) and we have binded all 3 parameters in the same order.

And then, read_sql_query() method of pandas is called with SQL query, connection, and parameters.

3.0. Executing/calling SQL queries and user stored procedures (USP)

In this recipe we will see how we can execute different type of SQL queries and User stored procedures (USP) using SQLALCHEMY connection and its execute() methods.

There are many ways or approaches to execute SQL queries and USP, specifically we will discuss the following approaches,

- ✓ approach: 1- execute SQL query without parameters and fetchall() results into pandas dataframe
- ✓ approach: 2- execute SQL query with parameters with parameters + rowcount
- ✓ approach: 3- execute USP with parameters + rowcount

sqlalchemy_03_execute.py

```python
import sqlalchemy as sa
from sqlalchemy.sql import text
import pandas as pd
import __connection_string_utils as csutils


connection_string = csutils.get_odbc_connection_string()


print('connect to sql and execute sql ...\n')


### create engine url and the engine
engine_url = sa.engine.URL.create("mssql+pyodbc", query = dict(odbc_connect =
connection_string))
engine = sa.create_engine(engine_url, fast_executemany = True)


###############################################################
##### approach: 1- execute SQL query without parameters and fetchall() results into pandas
dataframe
###############################################################
try:
    ### create a connection and execute the sql
    ### it automatically closes the connection
    with engine.connect() as connection:

        ### execute the sql query here
        query = 'SELECT * FROM dbo.customers_tbd;'

        results = connection.execute(text(query))
        df = pd.DataFrame(results.fetchall())

        print(f'\n1- execute SQL query without parameters and fetchall() results into pandas
dataframe...')
        print(df)
except Exception as ex:
    print(f'\terror: \n{str(ex)}')
```

```python
################################################################
##### approach: 2- execute SQL query with parameters with parameters + rowcount
################################################################
try:
    with engine.connect().execution_options(autocommit = True) as connection:

        ### execute the sql query here
        ids = '11, 12'
        sql = f"""DELETE FROM dbo.customers_tbd WHERE ID IN ({ids});"""

        records_deleted =  connection.execute(text(sql)).rowcount
        # connection.commit() ### notice this explicit commit

        print(f'\n2- execute SQL query with parameters with parameters + rowcount...')
        print(f'deleted records count: {records_deleted}')


except Exception as ex:
    print(f'\terror: \n{str(ex)}')


################################################################
##### approach: 3- execute USP with parameters + rowcount
################################################################
try:
    with engine.connect().execution_options(autocommit = True) as connection:

        ### execute the sql query here
        id = 14
        name = 'SQLALCHEMY'
        sql = "{call [dbo].[usp_update_tbd] (:id, :name)}"
        params ={'id': id, 'name': name}

        result = connection.execute(text(sql), params)
        records_updated = result.rowcount

        print(f'\n3- execute USP with parameters  rowcount...')
        print(f'updated records count: {records_updated}')
except Exception as ex:
    print(f'\terror: \n{ex}')
```

As you can see   that in this topic, we are using the 'with' statement to make the connection after preparing the SQL connection string, engine and all.

Now let discuss the approaches,

approach: 1- execute SQL query without parameters and fetchall() results into pandas dataframe

Let say we have a simple select statement in SQL to read or select the data also it is not taking any parameters.

We can execute this SQL query using execute() of connection and as per query this is going to return a dataset with 1 or more rows and multiple column so we can use the fetchall() method after executing the query and then this result can be converted into pandas dataframe as,

```python
try:
    ### create a connection and execute the sql
    ### it automatically closes the connection
    with engine.connect() as connection:

        ### execute the sql query here
        query = 'SELECT * FROM dbo.customers_tbd;'

        results = connection.execute(text(query))
        df = pd.DataFrame(results.fetchall())

        print(f'\n1- execute SQL query without parameters and fetchall() results into pandas
dataframe...')
        print(df)
except Exception as ex:
    print(f'\terror: \n{str(ex)}')
```

As noticed, the SQL query is taken into a string variable within single quotes and wrapped within text() method.

We are using execute() method of connection and taking result into a variable called results which is actually a cursor and so we used fetchall() method to take resutset and passing it into DataFrame() method of pandas.

approach: 2- execute SQL query with parameters with parameters + rowcount

We may have a SQL query command that takes parameters, we can execute the SQL command or query in different ways, one of which is just preparing the SQL query with in-build parameters using string format or concatenation. Here we have built the query by string format as,

```python
try:
    with engine.connect().execution_options(autocommit = True) as connection:
```

```python
    ### execute the sql query here
    ids = '11, 12'
    sql = f"""DELETE FROM dbo.customers_tbd WHERE ID IN ({ids});"""


    records_deleted =  connection.execute(text(sql)).rowcount


    print(f'\n2- execute SQL query with parameters with parameters + rowcount...')
    print(f'deleted records count: {records_deleted}')

except Exception as ex:
    print(f'\terror: \n{str(ex)}')
```

In this query the parameter is in where condition with 'IN' logical operator, Notice the variable 'sql' here.

By the SQL query, it is a delete statement to delete the rows from the database table. So, when this query will be executed it may affect the number of records and we can take this number of affected records by using 'rowcount' property.

You may ask that we have not committed this SQL operation or transaction explicitly, so notice the with statement, we have used the execution_option() method here and declared the sutocomit = True. Hence, it will commit the transaction automatically.

approach: 3- execute USP with parameters + rowcount

In this approach, we will discuss about executing an User stored procedure (USP) in SQL. The USP may or may not have input parameters.

In case if it is taking the input parameters, we must pass those parameters and in case if the USP does not need to have any parameters we should avoid passing the parameters.

Let say, we have an USP which is taking 2 parameters, the 'id' and the 'name', the USP is dbo.usp_update_tbd.

```python
try:
    with engine.connect().execution_options(autocommit = True) as connection:


        ### execute the sql query here
        id = 14
        name = 'SQLALCHEMY'
        sql = "{call [dbo].[usp_update_tbd] (:id, :name)}"
        params ={'id': id, 'name': name}


        result = connection.execute(text(sql), params)
        records_updated = result.rowcount
```

```
        print(f'\n3- execute USP with parameters  rowcount...')
        print(f'updated records count: {records_updated}')
except Exception as ex:
    print(f'\terror: \n{ex}')
```

Notice that the call to the USP is declared using the 'call' keyword and parameters are marked with colon placeholder.

If you investigate the definition of this USP, you will see that it is updating the records in the database based on some conditions, so we are taking the number of rows affected by using 'rowcount' property.

In this way, you can execute any SQL command with or without parameters. These were some of the approaches to execute SQL query.

4.0. Executing/calling SQL scripts using exec_driver_sql()

approach: 1- execute SQL query by 'exec_driver_sql()' function

In this topic, we will discuss about exec_driver_sql() method, this is special way of executing the SQL commands or queries.

Usually, this approach should not be used, but for learning purpose you can try it.

Let's, investigate the code,

sqlalchemy_04_exec_driver_sql.py

```python
import sqlalchemy as sa
import __connection_string_utils as csutils


connection_string = csutils.get_odbc_connection_string()


print('connect to sql and execute sql by exec_driver_sql() ...\n')


### create engine url and the engine
engine_url = sa.engine.URL.create("mssql+pyodbc", query = dict(odbc_connect =
connection_string))
engine = sa.create_engine(engine_url, fast_executemany = True)


##############################################################
##### approach: 1- execute SQL query by 'exec_driver_sql()' function
##############################################################
```

```python
try:
    ### create a connection and execute the sql
    ### it automatically closes the connection
    with engine.begin() as conn:
        conn.exec_driver_sql('DELETE FROM dbo.customers_tbd WHERE ID = 14')


        print(f"\n1- execute SQL query by 'exec_driver_sql()' function...")
        print('record with id 14 deleted')

except Exception as ex:
    print(f'\terror: \n{str(ex)}')
```

As you noticed, we are getting the SQL connection string from our custom utility module and the creating the engine URL and engine and then using the 'with' statement.

Withing the 'with' statement, we have called the begin() method of the engine that return the connection object.

The connection object has the method exec_driver_sql(), here we are passing the complete QL query to delete the records from the database table. There is no parameter passed here but you can pass the parameter if required (we have seen various ways to pass the parameters).

By using exec_driver_sql() method we can execute any SQL command.

5.0. Executing/calling SQL scripts using raw_connection()

approach: 1- execute SQL with parameters using 'raw_connection()'

In this topic we will discuss about 'raw_connectio' in sqlalchemy.In sqlalchemy, it is possible to create a raw connection and execute the SQL commands.

Raw connection is a special kind of connection, usually it is not used commonly but we can check it for learning purpose.

By using raw connection, we can create the cursor and then we can use this cursor object in the fashion of pyodbc.

`sqlalchemy_05_raw_connection.py`

```python
import sqlalchemy as sa
import __connection_string_utils as csutils


connection_string = csutils.get_odbc_connection_string()
```

```python
print("connect to sql and execute sql using 'raw_connection()' ...\n")

### create engine url and the engine
engine_url = sa.engine.URL.create("mssql+pyodbc", query = dict(odbc_connect =
connection_string))
engine = sa.create_engine(engine_url, fast_executemany = True)


############################################################
##### approach: 1- execute SQL with parameters using 'raw_connection()'
############################################################

try:
    usp = '[dbo].[usp_getdata_by_country_tbd] @country_name = ?'

    country = 'Singapore'

    connection = engine.raw_connection()

    cur = connection.cursor()
    cur.execute(usp, [country])

    print(f'result:\n {cur.fetchall()}')

    cur.close()
    print(f"1- execute SQL with parameters using 'raw_connection()'...")
    print('usp executed successfully.')

except Exception as ex:
    print(f'\terror: \n{str(ex)}')
```

As you can see that after getting SQL connection string and creating engine URL and engine, withing try block we have declared a variable 'usp', which is calling an USP that takes one parameter.

Notice that we are not using 'call' or 'execute' keyword.

Then we are creating raw connection using raw_connection() method of engine, it return the connection object.

Then we are creating the cursor using cursor() method of connection object.

This cursor object is used to execute the SQL commands in this case the USP with parameters. We are using execute() method of the cursor object and passing the SQL query to execute and the required parameters.

This USP return the resultset which is taken by fetchall() method of the cursor and then the cursor is closed. We can delete the connection object once we are done the execution of SQL commands to dispose the object and release the connection.

6.0. Updating the data in SQL Database table using pandas dataframe and update sql statement

approach: 1- updating the data directly from pandas dataframe using update sql statement

In this topic we will discuss about updating the records in the database table using the pandas dataframe.

We cannot update the records in the database table from the pandas dataframe itself, we are just preparing the dataframe with the required values/columns and aligning with the SQL update statement parameters.

We must align either the dataframe and its column names as per the SQL updated statement and its parameters or vice-versa.

Let say we have an update statement in SQL with the parameters marked by colon parameter name syntax as,

```
update_sql = """UPDATE dbo.customers_tbd
SET customer_name = :cutomername_p,
    customer_country = :cutomercountry_p,
    is_b2b_customer = :isb2b_p
    WHERE id = :custid"""
```

Notice, the parameter place holders and its name,

1. :customername_p
2. :customercountry_p
3. :isb2b_p
4. :custid

Now, we have a dataframe as (it may be the result set of a database table or from any source),

```
data = {'custid': [9, 10, 13],
        'custname': ['B', 'NEW CUSTOMER NAME', 'usp_customername'],
        'country': ['Argentina', 'usp_customercountry', 'usp_customercountry'],
        'isb2b':[False, True, True],
```

```
            'currency':['indian rupee', 'Russian Ruble', 'Chinese Yuan']}

    df = pd.DataFrame(data)
    print(df)
    print()
```

In this dataframe the following are the columns,

1. custid
2. custname
3. country
4. isb2b
5. currency

In the SQL update statement, we want to update the following columns,
1. customer_name
2. customer_country
3. is_b2b_customer
4. based on specified value by 'custid' in 'id' column

There is a need of 4 parameters as per SQL update stament, 'custid' is already available in dataframe columns, now let's manipulate the dataframe to drive the rest of the parameter columns as,

```
    # df['cutomername_p'] = df['custname'].apply(lambda x: x.lower())
    df['cutomername_p'] = ['customer 1', 'customer 2', 'customer 3']
    df['cutomercountry_p'] = ['America', 'India', 'Singapore']
    df['isb2b_p'] = [False, False, False]
    print(df)
```

To drive the above columns you can apply your business logic.

Now, the dataframe has all 4 parameter columns.
Then we must prepare the parameters to pass into the execute() method along with SQL update statement.
We can prepare the parameters as,

```
    df_to_dict = tuple(df.to_dict(orient = 'records'))
```

As you noticed, the complete row of the dataframe is converted into dictionary and finally tuple of dictionary and hence multiple parameters are prepared.

Now we can execute the SQL update statement.

The complete code is here,

```python
import sqlalchemy as sa
from sqlalchemy.sql import text
import __connection_string_utils as csutils
import pandas as pd


connection_string = csutils.get_odbc_connection_string()


print("connect to sql and update data ...\n")


### create engine url and the engine
engine_url = sa.engine.URL.create("mssql+pyodbc", query = dict(odbc_connect =
connection_string))
engine = sa.create_engine(engine_url, fast_executemany = True)


################################################################
##### approach: 1- updating the data directly from pandas dataframe using update.sql statement
################################################################


try:

    data = {'custid': [9, 10, 13],
            'custname': ['B', 'NEW CUSTOMER NAME', 'usp_customername'],
            'country': ['Argentina', 'usp_customercountry', 'usp_customercountry'],
            'isb2b':[False, True, True],
            'currency':['indian rupee', 'Russian Ruble', 'Chinese Yuan']}

    df = pd.DataFrame(data)
    print(df)
    print()

    # df['cutomername_p'] = df['custname'].apply(lambda x: x.lower())
    df['cutomername_p'] = ['customer 1', 'customer 2', 'customer 3']
    df['cutomercountry_p'] = ['America', 'India', 'Singapore']
    df['isb2b_p'] = [False, False, False]
    print(df)

    update_sql = """UPDATE dbo.customers_tbd
    SET customer_name = :cutomername_p,
        customer_country = :cutomercountry_p,
        is_b2b_customer = :isb2b_p
```

```python
        WHERE id = :custid"""

    update_statement = text(update_sql)


    df_to_dict = tuple(df.to_dict(orient = 'records'))


    with engine.connect().execution_options(autocommit = True) as connection:
        _ = connection.execute(update_statement, df_to_dict)


        print(f"1- updating the data directly from pandas dataframe using update sql
statement...")
        print('\t\tupdate records completed successfully.')


except Exception as ex:
    print(f'\terror: \n{str(ex)}')
```

So, all the dataframe columns are used to prepare the multiple parameters in this recipe, you can exclude the non-required columns y selecting the required columns only.

7.0. Inserting pandas dataframe into SQL Database table

In this recipe, we will discuss about inserting the records into database table directly from the pandas dataframe.

approach: 1- inserting the data directly from pandas dataframe

Let say we a pandas dataframe and we want to insert all the records in a dataframe into database table. We can do so directly from the dataframe, pandas provide this functionality.

There is 'to_sql()' method available to achieve this. It can insert the records into existing database table as well as create new table in database.

`sqlalchemy_07_insert_by_pandas_df.py`

```python
import sqlalchemy as sa
import __connection_string_utils as csutils
import pandas as pd


connection_string = csutils.get_odbc_connection_string()


print("connect to sql and insert data ...\n")


### create engine url and the engine
```

```python
engine_url = sa.engine.URL.create("mssql+pyodbc", query = dict(odbc_connect =
connection_string))
engine = sa.create_engine(engine_url, fast_executemany = True)


##############################################################
##### approach: 1- inserting the data directly from pandas dataframe
##############################################################

try:

    data = {'name': ['P', 'Q', 'R'],
            'country': ['India', 'Russia', 'China'],
            'isb2b':[True, True, False],
            'currency':['indian rupee', 'Russian Ruble', 'Chinese Yuan']}

    df = pd.DataFrame(data)
    df = df.rename(columns={'name': 'customer_name'
                            , 'country': 'customer_country'
                            , 'isb2b': 'is_b2b_customer'})

    df = df[['customer_name', 'customer_country', 'is_b2b_customer']]

    print(df)
    print()

    schema_name = 'dbo'
    table_name = 'customers_tbd'

    df.to_sql(name = table_name
                , con = engine
                , schema = schema_name
                , if_exists = 'append'
                , chunksize = 10000
                , index = False)

    print(f"1- inserting the data directly from pandas dataframe...")
    print(f'records inserted: {df.shape[0]}')

except Exception as ex:
    print(f'\terror: \n{str(ex)}')
```

As you can see that we must create an engine of sqlalchemy, it is used as connection to the to_sql() function,

We have prepared a pandas dataframe and have selected the required columns to align with the existing SQL database table.

Then we have have called to_sql() method of dataframe with mentioned parameters such as,

1. name – the name of the table
2. con – the sqlalchemy engine
3. schema – the schema of the table
4. if_exists – how to handle the insertion for example append, insert, etc.
5. chunksize – the number of rows to create chunks to perform insertion
6. index – whether index is true or false

There are other parameters also and for inserting the records in the existing table these are enough. To know more about this functionality and specifically this method to_sql() read the official documentation.

8.0. Executing SQL query in multiple databases using loop

In this recipe we will discuss how we can execute SQL query in multiple databases.

There may be a scenario where we have a SQL query and want to execute in a list of databases (multiple databases). This SQL query can be to create a table, to perform a DDL operation, or to perform a DCL operation, or even as simple as DML operation.

Most of the time, table, USP creation or deployment in multiple databases or deleting a table from multiple databases is the best scenario.

Here we will look at the following scenarios,

loop through databases: executing sql query in multiple databases

Let say, we want to create a table in multiple SQL databases as a deployment activity, we have a list of databases. Then we must iterate over the list of databases and prepare the SQL connection string and create the engine URL and the engine of sqlalchemy.
Then create the connection using engine and execute the SQL query in this case create table SQL statement.

`sqlalchemy_08_loopthrough.py`

```python
import sqlalchemy as sa
from sqlalchemy.sql import text
import __connection_details_sqlserver as sqldetails


#############################################################
##### loop through databases: executing sql query in multiple databases
#############################################################
```

```python
print('connect to sql and execute query ...\n')

list_dbs = ['db-customer1', 'db-customer2', 'db-customer3',]

for db in list_dbs:
    print(f'db: {db}')

    ### ### read details
    if 1 == 1:
        ### at least the following details
        DRIVER = sqldetails.DRIVER
        SERVER = sqldetails.SERVER
        DATABASE = db #sqldetails.DATABASE
        USERID = sqldetails.USERID
        PASSWORD = sqldetails.PASSWORD
        ### additional details
        ENCRYPT = sqldetails.ENCRYPT
        TRUSTSERVERCERTIFICATE = sqldetails.TRUSTSERVERCERTIFICATE
        CONNECTION_TIMEOUT = sqldetails.CONNECTION_TIMEOUT
        PACKET_SIZE = sqldetails.PACKET_SIZE

    ### prepare connection string here
    connection_string = f'''Driver={DRIVER};
Server={SERVER};
Database={DATABASE};
Uid={USERID};
Pwd={PASSWORD};
Encrypt=yes;
TrustServerCertificate=no;
Connection Timeout=1800;
Packet Size=4096;'''

    engine_url = sa.engine.URL.create("mssql+pyodbc", query = dict(odbc_connect = connection_string))
    engine = sa.create_engine(engine_url, fast_executemany = True)


    try:
        ### create a connection and execute the sql
        ### it automatically closes the connection

        with engine.connect() as connection:

            ### execute the sql commands here
```

```python
        ###############################################################
        ##### any sql command that you want to execute in the listed multiple databases
        ##### such as creating a table in all databases or deleting a table from all
databases
        ##### or shrinking the log file in all the databases, and so on
        ###############################################################

        sql = """CREATE TABLE dbo.currencies3_tbd(
            ID INT IDENTITY(1, 1),
            currency NVARCHAR(20) NOT NULL,
            currency_description NVARCHAR(20) NOT NULL,
        )"""

        ### execute the sql query here
        results = connection.execute(text(sql))
        print('\tquery executed successfully')

    except Exception as ex:
        print(f'\terror: \n{str(ex)}')
```

This is how we can deploy the common SQL objects or perform SQL operations in multiple databases by looping through the list of databases.

We must prepare the SQL connection string targeting the intended or current database and execute the SQL.

These were the few important recipes in PYODBC and SQLALCHEMY to work with data and databases specifically in Microsoft SQL Server. However we have prepared these recipes for working with Microsoft SQL Server, you can do the required adjustments in the code to work with other RDMS SQL Servers if the PYODBC & SQLALCHEMY supports those SQL Servers.

My environment setup

Windows Version:

Windows 11

Python version:

Python 3.8.13

```
(envpython38) C:\Users\oms\Desktop\2024\sqlwithpython>python --version
Python 3.8.13

(envpython38) C:\Users\oms\Desktop\2024\sqlwithpython>
```

pyodbc version:

```
pyodbc              4.0.34
```

sqlalchemy version:

```
SQLAlchemy          1.4.41
```

pandas version:

```
pandas              1.4.1
```

Contact

If you need any help to learn or understand SQL with Python or SSIS you can contact me by visiting my LinkedIn profile om shakya and follow us on LinkedIn page sql with python.

You can also contact me for full time or part time Python Data Engineering or SQL Development work outsourcing.
I will be very helpful and excellent fit for research and development (R&D) work or secret & private project or to develop custom tools.

www.ingramcontent.com/pod-product-compliance
Lightning Source LLC
LaVergne TN
LVHW081801050326
832903LV00027B/2036